Through Gypsy Eyes

Through Gypsy Eyes

Kathy Etchingham

with Andrew Crofts

VICTOR GOLLANCZ

LONDON

First published in Great Britain 1998
by Victor Gollancz

An imprint of the Cassell Group
Wellington House, 125 Strand, London WC2R 0BB

© Kathy Etchingham 1998

The right of Kathy Etchingham to be identified as author
of this work has been asserted by her in accordance with
the Copyright, Designs and Patents Act, 1988.

A catalogue record for this book is
available from the British Library.

ISBN 0 575 06619 9

All photographs courtesy of the author
unless otherwise acknowledged.

Typeset by Rowland Phototypesetting Ltd,
Bury St Edmunds, Suffolk
Printed in Great Britain by
St Edmundsbury Press Ltd, Bury St Edmunds, Suffolk

98 99 5 4 3 2 1

Acknowledgements

I would like to thank the late Chas Chandler for putting the idea of doing this book into my head. Thanks also to Jimi's biographer Harry Shapiro for his encouragement.

To Tony Brown a very special thank you. Also to Andrew Crofts for patiently listening and writing it all down.

Thanks to my husband Nick for all his love and support, and to all those too numerous to mention but who know they were all part of the story.

Prologue

As the taxi drew out of Grosvenor Square into Brook Street and I saw the size of the crowd up ahead, I felt suddenly anxious. Surely, I thought, we were too early. I went cold with terror.

'Ask him to stop for a moment,' I said to Nick, my voice sounding squeaky and unfamiliar in my ears.

'Can you pull over?' Nick asked the driver.

The driver drew in just past Claridge's and we stared down the road at the scene which awaited us: at the crash barriers and the police with their radios, at the cameras and the microphones and the throngs of onlookers who were spilling off the pavements and out of the designated areas into the street, forcing the traffic to a virtual standstill, each car having to be helped through to Bond Street by the police.

I took a few deep breaths and tried to stop myself from shaking. I had learnt my speech off by heart but had taken the precaution of asking Nick to run a copy off in large print – I didn't trust my voice to work in conjunction with my memory in front of such a huge crowd. If I could read it, I thought, I would be able to get through. Just a few hours before I had practically passed out in Selfridges while desperately hunting for a necklace to go with my outfit, leaving everything to the last minute as usual. The build-up of nervous energy from the previous months of frantic activity left me light-headed now that the time had finally come. All the hours I had spent in meetings, organizing the money, the security, the invitations and all the other details of such a big event had left me excited but drained. It was all so different to how things had been thirty years before when I first found the flat in Brook Street which was to become Jimi's and my home.

'OK,' I nodded to Nick, 'I'm all right.'

The driver drew out and we drove forward towards the crowds, my heart thumping in my chest.

The Blue Plaque to be unveiled was on the wall of 23 Brook Street, the house where Jimi Hendrix and I shared a flat together in the sixties. In the street outside barriers had been erected to allow invited guests to get close. Many of the media were inside the railings, while those without invitations hung from the windows opposite, trying to get a view of the proceedings.

Outside the barriers another group of the media clustered around the frail figure of Al Hendrix, Jimi's dad, and Janie Wright, the daughter of a Japanese woman Al married after Jimi had left America and come to England. Some wondered why Al wasn't in the VIP enclosure with the rest of us and Janie was telling the press that he hadn't been invited. I had handled all the invitations, I knew every detail of the administration, I knew that Al and Jimi's brother, Leon, had both been invited. I hadn't invited Janie because I didn't want the event to be turned into a promotional exercise for her company. There had been a furious exchange of letters and faxes over the previous months but I had remained firm. Fans, who I had invited over from America, overheard what Janie was saying and began to heckle her.

'You're lying!' they shouted, 'Al was invited!'

When the Hendrix family first won back control of his estate from the lawyers everyone had been pleased for them, but the mood of the fans changed once the family company, Experience Hendrix, started to merchandise things like $4,000 chairs with

Jimi's face on the seat, Hendrix rocking chairs and luminous Hendrix golf balls. They published stories saying that Jimi didn't die of a drug overdose and that the coroners, pathologists and the rest of us had got it wrong.

Even now, over a quarter of a century after his death, everyone still wants a piece of Jimi. Egos clash. The music industry of the sixties attracted a particularly colourful array of characters, many creative but others merely hangers-on. One of the reasons why I had suggested to English Heritage that they put up a Blue Plaque to Jimi was that London was the place where he had made his mark.

It didn't take them long to agree although Jimi was the first rock star they had ever honoured in this way. Once it was decided to go ahead, the unveiling quickly grew into a major event. There were some dissenting voices, notably Geoffrey Wheatcroft in the *Daily Express*, Brian Sewell, the art critic, and Clive Aslet, editor of *Country Life*, who thought that honouring a rock star meant English Heritage were 'dumbing down' and degrading the Blue Plaque tradition. Fortunately they were voices crying in the wilderness and everyone else agreed that it was a good thing.

Mojo magazine helped me throw a party afterwards for a few hundred people. It was difficult keeping the invitations out of the wrong hands. Every kind of freeloader and sponger seemed to want to be there and we had to keep security tight. There were faces there I hadn't seen in thirty years, survivors of the era when the Who sang 'Hope I die before I get old'. Jimi himself, of course, along with many of his generation had done just that, fuelling the myths and legends that surrounded 'Swinging London'.

There were also a lot of new young faces at the party from bands my teenage sons knew but who were a mystery to me. Several generations of musical talent have come and gone since Jimi and I set up home together in Brook Street, but still the musicians, the fans and the industry which profits from his back catalogue, turned out to honour him.

But even today, when so much of it has become history and the Handel Trust intends to recreate our old flat as a museum, past rivalries still rumble on. I had approached four guitarists who had known us to help with the unveiling: Pete Townshend, Jeff Beck, Jimmy Page and Eric Clapton. Pete and Jeff both said yes, but Jeff dropped out at the last minute. Jimmy Page didn't reply about doing the unveiling but said he would like to attend and Eric Clapton's people told me he was out of the country at the time. I was amazed by how many of our friends from the old days did not even bother to RSVP, while modern 'bad boys' like Oasis were the model of good manners and respect and did. Anyway, in the end, the Emporium Club in Kingly Street, better known to our generation as the Valbonne, positively heaved with famous faces, old and young, despite the fact that many on the guest list, such as Sting, were attending 'An Audience with Elton John' that evening. The McCartneys, unable to come because they were going to be on holiday, sent a huge bouquet of flowers and a message of goodwill to Jimi and everyone who had turned up.

Inside the Emporium, the speeches and photo sessions over, my nerves dissolved but I was still not able to relax as what seemed like hundreds of people I hadn't seen for years wanted to talk to me at once.

So much misinformation has been published and broadcast over the years about Jimi's short but spectacular life by people with an interest only in self-aggrandizement, that a few years ago I finally decided to break my silence of twenty years and record my version of events. This is not just a story about Jimi, but it's about me, and others who I knew in those early days and who are no longer with us, like Keith Moon, Brian Jones and Chas Chandler, and it's about what it was like to live in those extraordinary times.

1

I stood at the gate every day for three weeks, waiting for my mother to come home to get us like she promised. It was eerily quiet for most of the day, since there were no other children living in our row and hardly any traffic ever passed by. It gave me plenty of time to think.

'You still there, Kappy?' my dad would ask when the van dropped him home from work, hardly waiting for an answer before he disappeared into the house to get himself drunk.

When, eventually, after three weeks, my mother stepped down off the bus a few hundred yards away and I watched her walking back towards me, I was so relieved to see her that I didn't think to ask where she had been. She let herself into the house as if nothing had happened, with me bouncing joyfully at her side like an overexcited puppy. She had come back to us on her own, with no sign or mention of the wicked Tom. Everything was going to be all right again.

And for a few days it was all right. She went back to cooking and cleaning for us and we still didn't ask any questions. I just wanted to forget the whole thing and get on with life as before, but a few days later she was gone again, leaving our tea on the table, traces of her perfume on the sofa and a note to Dad saying she couldn't put up with him any more. This time the note made no promise about coming back.

I think I closed the doors to my heart at that moment, unwilling to let any more pain in. I didn't go back to waiting at the gate. Perhaps I knew that she wasn't going to change her mind and that it was now up to my brother John and me to look after ourselves. It was no good relying on her or anyone else, that was certain. These seeds of self-reliance would eventually grow to help me cope in an adult jungle which destroyed many of my friends. But at the age of ten I had no soil in which the seeds could thrive. I did not have the faintest idea how to get by without her.

John and I hadn't had any warning when she walked out and, of course, we knew nothing of our mother's past. If we had we might have been better prepared.

The first time she left we heard the row from upstairs and crept out of our bedrooms, sitting silent and shivering on the stairs in order to get a better idea of what was going on. There were three of them shouting: Lil, who I still called Mum in those days, Dad and our lodger, Con. Con's real name was Tom, and was sometimes known as Connie.

When John and I were tiny we all lived in the centre of Derby and Lil had been like any other mum, dressed in dowdy austerity clothes and occupying herself with the business of looking after two small children and a hopeless husband to whom nothing was ever a problem and yet who was incapable of achieving anything. Our house was in a terrace which had an entrance through the middle leading to small gardens at the back, and outside toilets which had to be emptied every so often by the council. A tin bath hung on the wall outside and would be brought into the kitchen on bath nights, put in front of the fire and filled with water boiled on the cooker. Today it sounds like poverty, the sort of genteel, picturesque poverty which the BBC likes to make drama series out of, but to us at the end of the forties it seemed a perfectly respectable way to live. Dad had some sort of engineering job at Rolls-Royce.

They were much older than everyone else's parents, which was a considerable embarrassment to me at school. Lil was approaching fifty. If on one of their rare visits to the school one of my friends asked me who they were, I would say they were my grandparents.

On Sundays Lil would cook a big family lunch and her mother, brother and stepfather would come round from 7 Raven Street, the house where I was born. Uncle Jack, who was at least twenty years younger than Lil, was a good-hearted but rather simple man whose destiny was to keep their mother company until the day she died. Family mythology held that some sort of accident at birth had starved him of oxygen and left him a bit different from everyone else, prone to making sudden loud and unexpected noises. If there was ever any danger that he would move away from home, my grandmother, who never allowed anyone to escape her clutches without a fight, would threaten to come back and haunt him once she was dead. He had a job at the ordnance depot in Derby and was always smartly dressed in a jacket and tie, no matter how informal the occasion. One of his roles was as his mother's chauffeur. Their cars always had fanciful names like 'Leaping Lena' and were treated like horses which had to be 'watered' every so often.

Everyone was afraid of my grandmother, a colossus of opinionated self-righteousness with a savage tongue, who my nephew and niece always referred to as 'Black Nana'. When I first challenged them about it they told me it was because of the colour of her hat. Eventually they admitted that it was more to do with her nature and swarthy features.

Her parents had been Romany gypsies from Hungary and there was still a lot of gypsy in Black Nana and Lil. They were very close at that time, forever poring over the tea leaves together at the kitchen table, arguing about what they could see in store

13

for us all. I remember being told I was going to marry a soldier and have four children. They tried to show me the pictures in the tea leaves.

'It's a car,' Lil would say, squinting into the cup.

'No,' Black Nana would overrule her, 'it's a horse.'

I would think it was just a bunch of sludge; it never made any sense to me.

They were full of superstitions about things like 'crossing your palm with silver' for good luck and visiting fortune-tellers and other clairvoyants. They used to take me to listen to mediums in a hall near the Trocadero in Derby. They would buy me a stick of liquorice to keep me quiet and then trail me in to listen to some theatrical old woman pretending to speak to the dead.

Even as a small child it all seemed transparently ridiculous to me, but I kept quiet; not that they would have taken any notice of anything I had to say, anyway.

Black Nana's parents, who didn't speak English, went into service when they came to England and she had followed the same line of work. Later she met my grandfather when working in a railway café. She was a wonderful cook, always making the sort of puddings children love. My grandfather died before I was born (Lil said she received messages and guidance from him until the day she died), and Black Nana's second husband was an enormously nice man called Jim Clarkin. Jim had been a vaudeville act and used to talk about how he had once trodden the streets of New York with Charlie Chaplin in search of work. The rest of them had never travelled abroad further than Ireland and never would. To me, Jim's tales of vaudeville and New York held out hope that there was a brighter, more exciting world outside the family.

When I was about five we moved out of town to Findon where Dad had got a job. We were completely isolated, just one row of council houses and a pub in the middle of nowhere, a few miles away from a power station.

Climbing trees was one of our favourite pastimes, as was playing marbles with the little glass balls from the Catseyes in the middle of the road. There was hardly any traffic in those days so we had plenty of time to gouge them out of their soft rubber sockets with penknives or kitchen implements without being spotted. We never had the money to buy marbles from shops and these had the added buzz of being stolen.

The only other building within walking distance was the corner shop which sold basic provisions like quarters of tea, bread, sweets and firelighters. All around was countryside.

A workforce had been assembled to build the power station, most of them recruited from Ireland, all of whom needed to find lodgings in the surrounding areas. That was where Tom had come from. There were also a few Fijians who Lil really liked because they were exotic and had money. She flirted with them outrageously.

Millie Eyre, the landlady of the pub, and Lil became good friends. Lil and Dad would go down there most evenings, leaving John and me outside with a packet of crisps and a bottle of lemonade. They never came out to check on us before closing time so we were free to do as we liked. We generally went 'down the cut', a Victorian canal nearby, with my dog, Lady, a Manchester terrier cross.

Millie's daughter, Sally, was a Down's syndrome child nearly the same age as me. She liked to play with the stones on the railway lines which carried the Flying Scotsman whistling past on its journeys up and down the country. She would sit there for hours, blissfully unaware of the potential danger. If ever she went missing they always knew where to look for her. I found her there one day and just as I saw her I heard the sound of the approaching train. I shouted at her to move but she took no

15

notice. I could see the front of the train coming round the corner and so I ran at her, screaming to make her move. She stood up and started running down the track ahead of the train, frightened by my angry voice. I ran after her but she was fast. The train was almost on us when I reached her, my lungs almost bursting with the effort, and yanked her to one side. The train sped past with a tremendous roar, the driver leaning out of the cab just feet away from us.

Millie Eyre was not like any mother I had come across up till then. She dyed her hair jet black, and wore make-up of the kind you only normally saw in magazines. She also had clothes which didn't look as if they had been handed down to her. Quite soon, under Millie's influence, my mother started looking the same. Perhaps that was the point at which she began to mutate from being Mum to being Lil, a woman who really should never have had children.

I suppose it must have been the real her re-emerging, because she told us that when she was a girl she had worked as a mannequin for Madame Lesley's, a couture shop in Derby, and pictures show that she was very pretty. The gypsy influence was more noticeable once she started to dress up with plunging necklines, pinched waists and flared skirts. All her tastes were bright and gaudy.

She was wearing one of her new dresses on the night that John and I saw her walk out, a bright yellow one covered in black roses. As I watched her go on Tom's arm the vibrant material was still visible long after her head and limbs had disappeared into the blackness of the night.

Tom was around twenty years old, at least thirty years younger than she was, when he came to live with us. John and I took the sudden appearance of a young lodger in our stride. He was just another grown-up to us, of no more interest than any of the others. When Tom and Lil took us for an outing, sending us down to the river to play, with Lady gambolling around our ankles, while they stayed in the car, we thought nothing of it. A ram in the field, however, objected to our trespassing on his territory and chased us back to where we had come from. John got to the car first and saw Tom and Lil kissing. He told me about it later, but I dismissed his stories as ridiculous.

From then on Tom seemed to be with us wherever we went, whether Dad was there or not. Our father was never one to put up much of a fight about anything, despite being Irish and partial to a drink, but John and I began to hear raised voices. This particular night, which brought us both out of our bedrooms and on to the stairs, was the worst ever, a frightening mixture of grief and anxiety from my father, belligerence and resentment from my mother and bravado from Tom. There was an ugly, drunken edge to the argument. Neither Tom nor Charlie ever raised their voices unless they had a drink inside them.

Tom and Lil burst out of the sitting room, my mother shouting, 'I'm going! I'm going! I'm leaving!' and swept out the front door with Tom, slamming it behind her.

'She's leaving me! She's leaving me!' Dad yelled pathetically up to us from the hall. John and I ran into the night after her, still in our pyjamas.

'Where are you going?' I shouted.

'I'll be back for you,' and then even the dress was gone. It never occurred to me that she might not mean it.

I stayed at the gate every minute I could, dashing in and out of the house if I had to eat or drink. Every time the bus stopped I held my breath, praying that she would be one of the people to step off. Each time it was someone else and I would feel my heart sink painfully in my chest. When I finally had to go to bed each night I continued watching from the window until the last bus had been and gone and I knew she wasn't coming back until the next day. As I lay staring at the ceiling I could hear

17

my father stumbling about the house as he tried to drown his hurt in booze.

Dad just about kept himself going during the three weeks until her return, but when she went the second time she took what little spirit he had left with her. He had no more idea how to look after John and me than we had of how to look after him. It was like leaving three small children together. He managed to get himself to work for a while, but by the time he came home he was too drunk to help us and would just have to sleep it off.

I missed her so much I would just lie on the sofa where I could still smell her perfume, the last reminder I had of her existence. John tried to take on the responsibility of looking after me as well as any twelve-year-old could hope to. He attempted to cook for us but we had no money and the local shop refused to give us any credit. I guess they knew all about our circumstances – perhaps Lil and Dad had run up bills in the past.

I think my grandmother probably gave Dad a little money for us but he must have drunk it away. Once they gave me twelve and six and sent me into town to buy myself a pair of sandals for school. They meant me to get the solid brown shoes with buckles that every other child had, but I had other ideas. They had said sandals, so I took them literally and bought a dainty, strappy little pair with wedge heels. I was so pleased with them I put them on immediately. Getting home involved a few miles of walking to and from buses so there was no way the shoes could go back to the shop. They were furious that I had wasted so much money. It hadn't occurred to them that a ten-year-old girl should be accompanied when she goes to buy shoes.

I remember John standing at the cooker stirring a pan of tomato soup and tasting it off the spoon.

'You put that in your mouth!' I accused him indignantly. 'You'll give me your germs.'

'It's a wooden spoon,' he assured me confidently, 'wood kills germs.'

There was a well under the kitchen which supplied us with our water through a pump. If there were heavy rains in the area we were supposed to pump up some of the water and send it away down the drains, but no one had told John or me that. The first we knew that something was wrong was when the water level rose up through the kitchen floor. We tried to empty the room with saucepans, but the level never seemed to drop. Dad was in no fit state even to call in the council, so we just had to wade around until the rains stopped and the level in the well went down.

Eventually Dad couldn't get himself out of bed most days and gave up work, or was sacked. Sometimes we couldn't wake him at all and he would just lie all day in sheets that were gradually growing grimier, snoring and spluttering and deaf to our voices until it was opening time at the pub.

We needed fuel for the fire and John had noticed that lumps of coal fell off the tenders of the steam trains as they went under a nearby bridge. So we climbed down to the sides of the track with Lil's old shopping bags to collect enough to keep ourselves warm. John and I grew very close during those weeks, clinging to one another for some semblance of security in a world where everyone had deserted us.

We would try to get out of the house in the evenings to play with Lady and take her for walks. We hung around with Nicky Eyre who was always stealing money from his father's till at the pub and was consequently a potential source of food. He used to torture us by buying bottles of pop and emptying them into the canal in front of our eyes, but sometimes he would steal bread for us from the pub kitchen and we were more than grateful for anything he passed on.

It must have been obvious to anyone who saw us that we were

in a bad way. John couldn't possibly take care of me and my clothes were becoming dirtier and tattier every day. Today if a child turned up at school in the state we were in the social services would be round within twenty-four hours, but no one took any notice then. I must have been suffering from malnutrition: clumps of my hair were falling out. My gums were bleeding from gingivitis.

One of the teachers took pity on me and gave me a bag of cast-off clothes, including one of her own dresses. It was blue with a sailor's collar but she was a normal-sized adult and the material hung almost to the ground on me, the sleeves covering my hands. Still, it was in a better state than anything I owned and so I wore it to school, with her giant plimsolls flopping on my feet, and suffered the jibes.

We both used to get a lot of teasing and trouble from the other children. I was called names like 'gyppo' and 'tinker' because of my grubby, ill-fitting clothes. Now I can see it was a form of racial abuse but as a child I simply felt angry and ashamed. I learnt to be more aggressive than anyone else in my attempt to protect myself from hurt. There was no one else in the school who looked like us. As far as the teachers were concerned both John and I seemed as well behaved as any of the other children despite our appearance, but in the playground I was fighting all the time. When the thought of sticking up for myself all day became too much I would just duck out of school and go down to the cut to play by myself or with John if I could persuade him to join me.

One evening in the pub Dad met a couple who said they would come and look after us for him, and of course he agreed. When they arrived they brought their four children with them and John and I found ourselves relegated to the bottom of the pecking order. It was obvious to both of us that they were not nice people and pretty rough, but Dad never noticed a thing. As long as they were willing to relieve him of his responsibilities he did not intend to ask any questions or make any demands of them. That would not have been the way to the quiet life he craved. One day we came home from school to find that Lady had disappeared from her kennel outside the back door.

'Where's Lady?' I screamed, 'where's my dog?'

To begin with they wouldn't tell me anything, then they said that she had been taken ill suddenly and the vet had been forced to put her down. The next day their Alsatian took up residence in Lady's kennel. It was obvious that nothing was safe and nobody could be relied on. I kept thinking that if only Lil knew what was happening she would come back and rescue us, but we didn't have any idea where she was.

I think Dad must have fallen behind with the rent because the cuckoos in our nest went to the council and requested that they take over the lease on the house. Dad, as obliging as ever, signed whatever papers they put in front of him and a few days later the three of us found ourselves homeless.

The whole family was shocked at the way Lil had run off and left us, and they could all see that Dad was incapable but no one could decide whose responsibility we were. To begin with my grandmother had resentfully hauled herself on and off three different buses to get from the centre of town to cook us a meal once a week, complaining all the time that she had enough to do with looking after her husband Jim and our uncle Jack without all this extra work at her age, and grumbling about the mess we made of the house. But once we were homeless the family had to do something to help.

'The trouble with Lil,' I overheard the adults saying to one another on numerous occasions, 'is that she just can't live in a house. There's too much gypsy in her soul and all she wants is a caravan.' None of them seemed to expect her to return, so

21

someone other than our father was going to have to be found to take care of us.

Initially we were sent to our maiden aunt Valerie, Dad's sister in Dublin, to live with her in her flat above a shop. The flat was one of the last remnants of the family fortune. My paternal grandfather, James, had been a house and land agent who did very well by buying up Protestants' houses cheaply when they were pushed out of Dublin in the twenties and thirties and then selling them at a profit. He had once owned a lot of the property in Baghot Street, right in the centre of town, but when he died my father and his brothers lost everything in a very short time. None of them were ever any good at coping with life. Dad always said it was because they had had the stuffing knocked out of them by the Christian Brothers at school, who were renowned for the continual beatings they meted out to their charges.

My father finally sold the last of his inheritance to a band of tinkers who he went to live with a few years later. They paid him £8,000 and today the buildings, including a row of Georgian houses, are part of a complex containing a McDonald's franchise.

The rest of the family were rather grand compared to us, well educated and living in nice houses. They looked down on us with undisguised contempt. Dad had further disgraced himself by marrying a non-Catholic, which meant that we were to be pitied as well as despised.

Never having even married, much less had children of her own, Aunt Valerie found our arrival something of a shock. She was enormously tall and thin, with a sort of goitre sticking out of her neck. She always smelt dirty and never seemed to spend any time in the bathroom. We caught a glimpse of her feet once and they were encrusted with dirt. Never having had to cook because she had been brought up with servants, she fed us nothing but salty porridge and potatoes, which she boiled in their skins. She took us to church twice a day. Before long John and

I realized that something had to be done if we weren't going to die of her cooking or boredom.

We hatched a plot to escape. We caught a bus to the ferry at Dun Laoghaire and, by pretending to be part of a family group, we managed to get on board without tickets. Throughout the voyage we moved surreptitiously from one group to another in the hope that no one would notice we were travelling on our own. It felt wonderful to be free of Aunt Valerie, although we had no idea what we would do once we arrived in England. We were just trusting to luck and enjoying the adventure as we went. Perhaps John imagined he would get a job and be able to support us. We didn't really give the future much thought, we just wanted to escape from that dreadful flat and taste freedom again. As the boat reached Holyhead we were both ecstatic, believing we had got away with it, and we waited impatiently as the docking process ground on and the gangway was lowered. But someone on board must have noticed us darting furtively around and alerted the authorities because the police were waiting for us as we disembarked.

We were not up to spinning yarns or giving false addresses. We confessed who we were the moment we were asked. Dad was duly contacted and the family had to think again. I imagine Aunt Valerie was as reluctant to have us back as we would have been to go. Something more suitable had to be thought of. It was decided that together we were too much trouble. We would have to be separated since there wasn't anyone in the family who could handle both of us. As I was a girl, and the youngest, I was deemed the one most in need of pastoral care. John, it was decided, could keep going with Dad for the time being.

We had a half-sister nineteen years older than us, called Jean, who I knew was the product of a marriage my mother had made before she met Dad, although I was unsure of the details. Everyone seemed to go very quiet and change the subject whenever Lil's past came up for discussion and I was never sufficiently interested to pursue it. Jean was rather plain-looking. She always seemed slightly jealous of me, referring to me rather bitterly as 'the pretty one' and pointedly turning my photo to the wall whenever she went round to visit Lil.

It fell to Jean, however, to look after me next. She had two small children and a husband called Edwin who worked as a psychiatric nurse at the local mental hospital. Being parted from John was a terrible wrench and I discovered many years later that he was just as traumatized by the separation. He spent the next few years being dragged around behind Dad from one scruffy boarding house to the next, sometimes having to share dormitories with other Irish working men as they struggled to survive. From then on no one ever called me Kappy. I became known as Kathleen.

I felt so emotionally vulnerable that whenever Edwin ordered me about in his gruff manner I took it personally and believed he was picking on me. Inside I became more and more tightly wound, more and more defensive as they tried to make me behave as they wanted. I told my grandmother that Edwin wasn't being kind to me and she must have said something to him which made the whole thing even worse. Not only was I a burden to them, I was now an ungrateful, treacherous burden.

Jean was very musical. She used to have a little record player and would play old dance tunes from the forties, tapping round the room to the music. She played the piano as well, which greatly impressed me. For the first time I realized that music offered an escape from the more humdrum elements of life. It lifted my spirits and helped me forget the real world.

Jean and Edwin lived in a close of council houses and Jean seemed to be forever falling out with her friends and neighbours. She didn't want me there and I didn't want to be there. We were two headstrong characters on a collision course and quite soon she decided that I was more than she could cope with. Dad had to make alternative arrangements again.

I think Aunt Lil was my grandmother's niece and she lived with her husband George, a kindly baker who worked nights. They had a daughter but she was grown-up with a family of her own, so it had been a long time since they had had to look after a child in their neat, clean little house. Aunt Lil's great passion was gambling and playing cards, so my life became an endless stream of other people's sitting rooms, where I would be sat down in a corner with a book for long evenings while Aunt Lil and her social circle got down to the serious business of pontoon. I particularly remember one room behind a furniture shop, where I managed to grab a few hours' sleep before it was time for school again.

Aunt Lil's other love was a pair of budgerigars which she kept in a cage in the parlour, constantly clucking over them and covering them at night with a black cloth so they would sleep better. I have never been very good with birds. I don't mind looking at them from a distance, or feeding them in the garden, but I am not comfortable if they come flapping around me. Aunt Lil liked to give her budgies the freedom of the parlour.

One day I was sitting on their beautifully kept sofa when Joey landed on my shoulder, his wings fluttering against my face. In shock I grabbed him and he dug his beak deep into my thumb. My initial panic was mixed with anger. I squeezed, and kept squeezing until the little blue and yellow body wasn't squirming any more and I could extract the sharp beak from my flesh.

Confronted with what to do with the body of my victim, I panicked all over again and rolled the wrung-out little corpse back into the cage, where it lay on the floor looking horribly incriminating. I was sure they would find out it was me, which would confirm in everybody's minds just what a terrible child I was, but I couldn't bring myself to own up to such a dastardly deed. When the body was found there was terrible grief, and not a little puzzlement, but amazingly, no one suspected who the murderer might be.

A few months after I had gone to live with Lil and George their daughter June came running to the house. The adults all bustled into the sitting room and shut the door in my face. I tried hard to hear what was going on but could only piece together fragments. It seemed that June's fireman husband had been arrested by the police for indecent exposure. I didn't know what that meant, but I knew it was something serious. It seemed certain he would lose his job. Obviously the shock was terrible. It was decided that there was a limit to how much adversity one family could cope with at one time. Another home would have to be found for me.

With each change in circumstances I was put into a different school. I coped with the pressure of having to make new friends and deal with new teachers by becoming moody and aggressive. I was not an easy child to live with.

My aunt Kathleen had married Dermot, a well-to-do man and lived in a big Georgian house called Eagleville in the suburbs of Dublin. Her daughter, Colette, who was a few years older than me, took exception to my arrival and even more to the idea of my sharing her room. So I was relegated to sleeping on a bed they set up in the rather splendid first-floor drawing room, which was fine by me. The family lived all the time in their kitchen and a room they called the parlour, which was stuffed with family silver and antique furniture. None of the children liked me.

At least Aunt Kathleen took me straight to see a dentist who saved my teeth, although I ended up losing a small part of my lower gum and had to have a skin graft. She also thought that something had to be done about my lack of education. It was decided that a convent would be the best place for me and I was enrolled at the Convent of the Holy Faith, a rather academic day school.

The nuns soon realized that because of my past I couldn't keep up with my peer group. They put me down a year but I still wasn't able to cope, so they suggested I went to their boarding school in Skerries. This led to a heated family debate about money and later Dad claimed that it was the need for school fees which drove him to sell the last of his inheritance to the gypsies for a song.

However it was financed, I was dispatched to Skerries and no doubt the entire family heaved a collective sigh of relief. No one had heard a word from Lil.

2

The nuns, another set of strangers, became my new family and the grey, cold, echoing corridors of the convent became my home. In a way I was quite glad to be away from Aunt Kathleen's two boisterous teenage sons who had teased me at every opportunity and Colette, who didn't even try to hide her resentment towards me. But I missed her dogs and my outgoing uncle Dermot who was a maker of religious cards and used to pay me to fold them and put them into envelopes for him.

I was beginning to find that I preferred being left to my own devices. I did not need other people around me, they only let me down. I liked being part of a crowd, but I didn't want to have to rely on anyone else for anything in life. I intended to look after myself in every way, just as soon as I was able.

Realizing that I might be trouble they put me next to the nun's cubicle in the dormitory and I set about getting used to the routine of starting and ending each day with prayers and a wash in cold water. Actually, the regime wasn't that different to Aunt Valerie's, but at least I had the company of other girls my own age and the food was better. Maybe it was bleak and depressing but it was no worse than anything else that had happened to me since Lil had disappeared.

Aunt Kathleen soon decided that it would be better if I stayed at the convent during the holidays as well as term time, as she had enough on her plate looking after her own children. My more or less orphan plight must have touched the sisters because while they frequently punished other girls for real and imagined crimes, smacking the backs of their bare legs with leather belts, they were always very merciful to me. They insisted that no one ever made fun of my situation, or pointed out that I never received any mail from anyone and possessed no photographs of family members. They also turned a blind eye when I cheated at hockey and cracked the opposition around the shins.

The sisters and the lay teachers gave a lot of their own time to help me with extra work. It was nice to have so much attention and I think I responded fairly well to their efforts. Any education I managed to pick up in life was due to them and I was eager to work hard whenever the opportunity arose. There had to be some sacrifices, however, in order to help me catch up in the most important subjects. As a result I never learnt to cook, a failing that grew into a mental block and was pointed out to me a great deal as an adult, causing a number of huge rows with various partners.

God began to play a major role in my life, since I figured his followers were the only people willing to give me any time at all. The sisters were determined to do all they could to save my soul and had me confirmed. They even went as far as making all the clothes I needed themselves, including a hat, and taking me off on the bus to the church in Dublin. At thirteen I was considerably older than all the other children being confirmed that day, and felt very self-conscious about my size. I confided my unease to sister Mary-Thérèse who was accompanying me, and who always smelt of stale urine.

'If they ask you,' she said after a moment's thought, 'just tell them you grew more than the others.'

During the holidays the nuns were especially kind to me. I remember them bringing me eggs one Easter and the local priest gave me a little medallion with my name on it. Mother Superior used to give me extra lessons in her study when all the other children were away, mostly to do with religious knowledge. Religion began to seem very attractive, giving me something to cling to in my unhappiness, some hope that there might be a great plan to all my suffering. I flirted with the idea of becoming a nun. I worked very hard to please them all.

Across the road from our dormitory window was the main hotel for the area and I used to spend hours watching people arriving in their smart clothes, getting out of their cars and going in to parties. Through the hotel's windows I could catch glimpses of the guests dancing in their evening gowns or talking in animated groups, and I dreamed of what life must be like for grown-ups who could go where they wanted and do as they pleased. Life looked so much fun once you were actually allowed to join in, when you could no longer be ignored or treated as nothing more than a burden and a nuisance that had to be hidden away until the whole childhood problem had disappeared.

At one stage the nuns decided we should be given the opportunity to learn ballet and they imported a teacher. We were all kitted out but I was the only person who didn't have any ballet shoes, so the sisters went out and bought some for me. Little acts of kindness like that made a big impression on me. We all became ballet-mad for a while, but I was so appalling, totally lacking any sense of rhythm or balance, that they must have decided it wasn't worth going as far as making me a dress.

I had been at the convent for more than a year when a lay teacher called me out of class one day. 'There's someone to see you with Mother Superior,' she told me. This was the first visit I had received since arriving and I couldn't imagine who it might be.

When we got to the office the Mother Superior came out and took me to one side. 'This may be a bit of a shock to you,' she said, her face full of concern. 'There's somebody here who wants to see you and there's nothing we can do to prevent it.'

She pushed open the door and there sat Lil, all dressed up in a conservative coat and hat. I hadn't seen her for four years. She jumped out of her chair and ran across the room. As she threw her arms round me I felt every muscle in my body stiffen at the unfamiliar physical contact, my arms pinned to my side and shoulders rigid with confusion, completely unable to tell if I felt happy to see her or horrified. I had no idea how to react.

'Oh Kathleen, how are you?' she gushed. 'It's been so long and I've missed you.'

I couldn't find any words with which to respond, my tongue and throat were frozen with shock. The Mother Superior gently withdrew to leave us alone together and Lil babbled away. I noticed that she kept talking about 'we' and I wondered what that meant. Was she still with the man Tom, the monster I had seen her disappear into the night with all those years before? Over the years I had carefully blocked out all thoughts of him, imagining my mother living alone somewhere, and I felt uneasy at the prospect that Tom might be coming back into my life as well. I put the thought out of my head and tried to concentrate on the pleasurable feeling of having my mother actually come to visit me.

'Is there anything you need?' she asked eventually.

I shrugged. 'Well,' I said after a moment, 'I need some new shoes, I suppose.'

'Let's ask them if you can come out shopping with me for a while,' she suggested. I nodded and she put the idea to the Mother Superior when she came back in, promising that she would return me to the convent later, saying exactly which bus we would be catching back out from Dublin. Mother Superior agreed, although I could sense that she wasn't comfortable about

31

it. I guess she didn't want to have to tell me that I couldn't enjoy this day as much as possible.

By the time we reached Dublin and had bought some shoes at a department store in O'Connell Street, I was beginning to thaw. It felt good to think that my mother had returned and was actually taking me out shopping. It made me feel more like other girls my age. Once she could see that I was having a good time she asked me a question. 'How would you like to come and live with me again?'

'Oh, yeah,' I enthused, 'that would be great!'

'We can send you to the local Roman Catholic convent,' she said, aware that I was now quite heavily religious, 'in Chester, where we live.'

'OK,' I said. I liked this idea even though I had spotted that another 'we' had slipped in.

'We can't go back to the convent in Skerries,' she said, thoughtfully, 'because I don't think they will agree to you going with me just like that. There's bound to be all sorts of boring formalities to go through. We don't want to bother with all that, do we?'

'No.' I didn't really understand what she meant but I felt excited at the thought of setting out on an adventure with her. 'What should we do, then?'

'I've got a ticket here for you,' she patted her handbag, 'for the ferry to England. So if we make our way there we can catch the next one and go home this afternoon.'

I still wasn't sure who we might be going home to. I kept hearing the dreaded 'we' in her conversation but I was too frightened of receiving the wrong answer to ask outright what she meant. I wanted to prolong the time we had together, just her and me, for as long as possible. Once we were safely on the ferry, however, our bridges burning merrily behind us, she told me that she was now living with Tom and that we would be like a family again. This confirmation of my suspicions made me go cold inside. Our short time alone was over already, the dream dead only a few hours after it was born. I wanted to be with her but I didn't want anything to do with the man with whom I associated the destruction of my childhood.

When we finally got to their little terraced house in Phillips Street, Chester, Tom was waiting and anxious to be as nice as possible to the stepdaughter he was about to inherit. I was sullen and not encouraging.

'I'll make you a nice cup of tea,' he said and sat us down at the kitchen table. I didn't speak, my throat tight with tension and apprehension. When the tea came I gulped at it and the hot liquid shot down the wrong way, sending me into a choking fit. As they rushed around patting me on the back and shouting instructions on how to get breathing again, I struggled for air, convinced that Tom was trying to kill me. Quite obviously he didn't want to live with me any more than I did with him.

Although I didn't die from choking, I convinced myself that he would try again. I became terrified of this harmless man, pinning a crucifix and a picture of Jesus above my bed to protect myself from him. If ever he came into my room, trying to be friendly, I would shrink back from him like a dog expecting a whipping, desperately working out how I would escape from his clutches if he suddenly lunged at me.

When we didn't return to the convent in Skerries on the designated bus that evening the nuns were sent into a complete spin, feeling themselves responsible for allowing me to be stolen by the scandalous Lil. News reached my father and in a rare burst of angry energy, he set out to search for me. He arrived in Chester with the name of the street but no number and wandered from house to house, banging on doors, asking if anyone knew where we were. He got as far as our next-door neighbour before Lil was alerted and went out with Tom to confront him.

33

'You stay there,' she ordered me, 'I don't want him snatching you away.'

I listened to all the screaming and shouting from inside the house. Shivering and anxious, I didn't know what was going to happen. I wanted to stay with Lil but I didn't want to be with Tom. I didn't want to go with Dad and I didn't particularly want to go back to being in the convent with no family at all, although at that moment it seemed the most peaceful option.

Dad was never any match for Lil – he didn't have the strength of will to put up more than a token fight, and that was probably fuelled by alcohol. When he realized he couldn't get anywhere he disappeared as suddenly as he had appeared, his tail between his legs. Aunt Kathleen, however, was not so easily defeated. She knew better than to take Lil on in a slanging match and turned to the law, applying to have me made a ward of court, hoping the judge would order me back to Skerries where at least I would be guaranteed an education and would be protected from the vagaries of Lil's mothering instincts. The court, however, decided differently. Lil emerged triumphant.

The convent my mother had promised to send me to in Chester was out of the question as soon as she realized how much the fees were. As well as coming to find me, she had also managed to re-establish contact with my grandmother and was making a brave attempt at rebuilding the family life which she had hated so much a few years before. I was enrolled at a rough Catholic secondary modern and Lil got an evening job in a pub to help make ends meet.

That was, effectively, the end of my education since the school appeared to be populated by delinquents and I was more than ready to be led astray. There was no one here to impress by working hard and I could see little point in making the effort. I was ready to start the adventure of adult life and the school represented another annoying delay. I began running away at every opportunity. I might have had my mother back, but whatever feelings I had imagined were there before I now knew had vanished. When you have nothing but childish memories to work with you can turn even Lil into an attractive mother figure. Confronted with the reality, I wanted to walk away from her just as she had walked away from me. I didn't trust her not to leave again. She was always threatening to, and all the resentments that had been bubbling away inside me since she had left now rose to the surface.

Maybe I still loved her because she was my mum, but I didn't believe any of her protestations that she would have come for me sooner if she had only had somewhere to live. I eventually found out that she had been living in caravans ever since leaving Dad, just as everyone in the family said she would. She must have moved into a house simply to make herself look more stable so that she would stand a better chance of getting me back if it came to a fight.

The effort of living in one place was almost more than she could bear. 'I can't stand it any longer!' she would scream loud and often, 'I'm tearing my hair out!'

As soon as I was out of the way she went back to the caravans. They might have been mobile homes, in fact, but she viewed them as romantic gypsy caravans like the ones in which her ancestors travelled around the Mediterranean during the last century. She was always very scathing about the Irish tinkers who would sell lucky heathers in the city centres, claiming that they were not real Romanies like her family.

In the end she was constantly moving from one site to another, always in search of somewhere new where life would be better – the true gypsy spirit showing up in her again. She would decorate all her homes in the same way, smothering them in shiny horse brasses and putting frills on every corner, edge and shelf that she could find.

She didn't have any idea what had happened to John since she left and didn't seem to be making any effort to be reunited with him. Perhaps the reality of having one child around the house again reminded her of why she had run away in the first place. She must have been as disappointed with the daughter she had got back as I was with her. When she had last seen me I was an affectionate, pliant little ten-year-old; now I was a belligerent, screwed-up, resentful adolescent.

At school Kathleen, the little convent girl, disappeared and I became known as Kate. I made a couple of good friends, one called Cynthia and another called Plum. Both Lil and Tom tried to exercise parental control over me, but it was impossible. They had made me too resilient; what could they possibly do to me that was worse than what they had done before? Apart from resorting to physical beatings, which was not in either of their natures, there was no punishment they could threaten me with. They couldn't take anything away from me because they hadn't given me anything. They couldn't shame me with their disapproval or disappointment at my behaviour because I had no respect for them. All they could do was complain about how much I was making them worry and how much trouble I was causing them. Such pleadings did not impress me. I now felt confident that I could make decisions every bit as good as theirs, and probably better.

I particularly resented Tom for trying to exert authority over me when it was his fault, in my eyes, that my whole family was in the state it was. As I got older they told me I had to be in by ten o'clock at night, but I would saunter in whenever I felt like it. They would be out in the streets looking for me and we would have screaming matches in front of the neighbours. I guess I had what would now be called an attitude problem.

My friend Plum was huge in body and personality: outgoing, honest and funny, just the sort of person I enjoyed being with and I let her sweep me along in her wake. Walking home from school, she used to make Cynthia and me laugh so much that we would wet ourselves. Her mother was doing her best to bring up Plum and innumerable brothers and sisters on the council estate on her own. They had no money and no possessions and their mother had no time, but I envied Plum the fact that she had a family who loved her. I was always envious of anyone who had a family set-up which was even partly functional, and would adopt them as my own given half a chance.

Cynthia was Anglo-Indian and from a rather better-off family than ours. She shocked us one day by lifting a purse out of the teacher's handbag when we were queuing up at the desk to have our work marked. In the break afterwards she told us excitedly what she had done. We were mortified. Fresh out of a convent, I felt sure she would be struck down by a thunderbolt before lunchtime, and us along with her as co-conspirators.

Once the crime was discovered we were each interrogated and I felt myself torn between my loyalty to a friend and my duty to Jesus, who was staring down at me accusingly from the wall as I mumbled my responses to their questions. They must have seen the guilt written all over my face because I was kept back after class and questioned again. Unable to withstand such concerted moral pressure I told them I knew who it was but wouldn't furnish them with the name. They didn't let me off with that. When the pressure grew too intense I cracked. Cynthia was expelled.

A few days later Lil received a letter from Cynthia's mum, asking us to pay her a visit. When we rolled up at their rather nice house, Cynthia's mother told us how this incident was quite out of character for her daughter, that it was myself and Plum's influence on Cynthia which had led her astray and that she knew all about my background. Lil was ferocious in my defence, possibly because she felt that such accusations reflected on her own abilities as a mother, and the matter never went any further.

Cynthia's departure meant that Plum and I were now on our own in our conspiracies to run away in search of adventure. I loved the feeling that I was starting to be in control of my own life, that I could actually have some fun and other people couldn't always stop me. In my own eyes I was almost an adult and I couldn't wait to make the final transition. Annoyingly the grown-up world still didn't seem to see me as an equal.

One thing about being shunted around as a child among people I didn't know was that it gave me confidence. I was never afraid of people, quite happy to walk up and talk to anyone. I was never able to understand those who lacked self-confidence in that area. It's still a mystery to me even today.

When we were planning one of our adventures Plum and I would meet at the bus stop in the morning, wearing school uniform, with our ordinary clothes in our bags and our dinner money in our pockets. We would change our clothes and then set off to the station, taking trains to wherever their destination might be. We never bothered to buy tickets but we never got caught. Ticket-collection systems can't have been very effective in those days.

We had romantic ideas: we would find a bedsit together in some distant city, get jobs and nobody would know how old we were. Usually we only lasted one night before the police would find us and bring us home for another round of rows. On one trip we got to Liverpool and, after wandering around the streets for a while, found an unlocked houseboat. We smuggled ourselves on board and settled down to cook ourselves some baked beans, but it wasn't long before the police turned up and frightened us with tales of how we would be charged with theft – of the baked beans – and breaking and entering. We hadn't done any damage so the owner didn't want to press any charges (the houseboat was unlocked and we hadn't had a chance to eat the beans) and we were sent home to more lectures.

'You'll be the death of me,' Lil would wail whenever I was brought back home, somehow forgetting that she had managed to let four years slip by without knowing or caring what was happening to me. Perhaps it was a question of 'out of sight, out of mind'. She and Tom gave up coming out to look for me at night and whenever I crept back into the house after curfew she would shout at me from their bedroom, 'Kathleen, is that you? What time do you call this?' I didn't bother to answer. I didn't plan to be there much longer.

Eventually Plum and I managed to get the train all the way to London. This was a place I knew I wanted to be. As far as I was concerned, this was the centre of the world.

Someone recommended a club in Soho's Gerrard Street, in the heart of buzzing Chinatown, where supposedly young people could go without being hassled and asked questions. It was a basement and there was a guy playing a saxophone. It was such a great sound, so haunting amid the bustle and excitement of the crowd that it took my breath away. We hadn't been sitting there long before I felt a tap on my shoulder. I turned to find the unglamorous figure of a policewoman standing over me.

'How old are you?' she asked.

'Sixteen,' I said.

'No you're not. I think you'd better come with me.'

There were a number of other under-age kids there and once the police ascertained that we were all runaways they took us off to Savile Row station, putting us into cells while they made their enquiries. This really put the wind up us as we imagined being taken into care and stuck in children's homes. It was a long night when nobody came to see us to ease our escalating worries.

The next day they split Plum and me up and sent us to two

different homes. I was dispatched to one in Norwood. There were a lot of hard kids there, and others who were badly messed up psychologically, just sitting in corners shaking all day. For me it wasn't too bad. I was there for three weeks and during that time I did things I had never done before, like play tennis. We used to spend a lot of time just sitting around talking about what was likely to happen to us next. Some of the kids had gone much further off the rails than Plum or I had the courage for, and listening to them talk I began to think that perhaps going home wasn't such a bad option. It wouldn't be long before I was old enough to come to London legally.

At the end of the three weeks I had to appear before a juvenile court. My family would have to demonstrate that they could provide me with the sort of home and support needed to keep me on the straight and narrow.

Uncle Jack was talked into driving Lil, Tom and Black Nana down to London in Leaping Lena, but when he reached Hyde Park Corner, which in those days had no traffic lights and was famous for being a bit of a race track, he had a panic attack, stopped the car and refused to go any further. None of the others was willing to take over the wheel as streams of traffic swerved all around them, the unsympathetic drivers honking their horns and shaking their fists, so they decided to abandon Lena and escape on foot. Mustering as much dignity as they could, they resumed their journey to the court on public transport.

A couple of hours later we were all sitting at a table in the giant courtroom. I was wearing a demure outfit Lil had sent down for me, trying to look like a dutiful daughter rather than a habitual runaway. The officials on the other side of the table asked me what I wanted to do.

'I want to go home,' I said, as plaintively as I could manage.

'Will you be trying to run away again?'

'Oh no.' I think I might have managed a catch in my voice at this point, if not a touch of water in the eyes.

Then it was Lil's turn to convince them that she could handle me if they let me return. She managed to pull it off – she could be pretty convincing when she put her mind to it, as the nuns in Skerries had discovered – and a few hours later, having rescued Leaping Lena from the police pound and paid the fine for abandoning her, we were all heading back up north.

I stared sulkily out of the car window while my grandmother gave me the tongue-lashing of a lifetime: what a wicked person I was, all the trouble I'd put them to, the worry I'd caused them, the expense of the trip, the embarrassment they had suffered, the worry for my poor mother, the worry for her . . . The others chipped in from time to time.

'Your grandmother's quite right.'

'You listen to your grandmother!'

'You're a selfish, wicked girl.'

I kept my eyes on the bleak roadside scenery and remained silent, dreaming of the day when I would be able actually to walk away and not be brought back in a car which had a horse's name.

'Who's that?' I asked, holding up a picture of two little girls. I was looking through some of my half-sister Jean's photograph albums.

'Anne and Davina,' Jean said, matter-of-factly, 'my sisters.'

I couldn't grasp what she was telling me.

'I had two,' she said, 'but they didn't come with Lil when she left our dad.'

'I don't understand, you mean I have two more half-sisters?' I said, and Jean sighed, sitting down beside me.

'When Lil was married to George, my dad, she had me, and then, much later, she had Anne and Davina. Here,' she turned up a picture of a young Lil in an expensive fur coat standing beside a prosperous-looking man in front of a Rolls-Royce. 'He'd done all right. He was a pharmacist and he had invented some sort of patent medicine. They had a big house and servants and everything, but Lil could never live in a house for long. Anyone else would have said she'd done well for herself marrying a man like my dad, but Lil got bored and ran off with the coalman, who was much younger than her.'

'What, just upped and went?'

'She went for three weeks to start with, then came back for me. I was about sixteen, but she left Anne and Davina with Dad. She's never had anything to do with them from that day on. No contact at all.' I was stunned. Everything Lil had put us through had happened before.

'What happened to the coalman?'

Jean shrugged. 'I don't know. The next thing was she married your dad – he was the lodger in your grandmother's house – and had you and John. Ten years later she repeated the whole performance with Tom.'

Jean was obviously shocked and upset that history had repeated itself, and that she, with two young children of her own, had been left to pick up the pieces. As for me, I just wanted my mother back. I would have forgiven her anything.

Lil finally managed to lure John away from Dad once he was old enough to make up his own mind. He lived with us for a while, working in a nearby bakery, but by then all the bonds of our early times together had been broken. We had both learnt to look after ourselves and to avoid being hurt by others. We had closed in on ourselves and didn't let others get too near. In fact, John teased me a lot when he came to live with us again.

Before long he joined the merchant navy and disappeared to New Zealand where he met a girl and jumped ship. When he finished with the girl she blew the whistle on him to the police and he was deported back to England. He got a job, saved enough money to pay for his own passage and went back down under, living for a while in the back of a disused car on a tomato patch. Eventually he became very successful as a nurse, educating himself in law and accountancy and settling permanently in Australia.

When I turned fifteen we moved back to Derby to be nearer to Black Nana. I think she must have bought my mother a house because I don't know how Lil could have afforded it any other way.

I left school and got myself a job in a shoe shop at three pounds, six shillings a week. It was terrible drudgery and confirmed my belief that I wanted something different out of life. All the other women there seemed to expect things to stay the same for ever. One of them had been at the shop for about thirty years, going out every lunchtime to buy food for her husband's supper. I vowed never to become like that.

It was in the shoe shop that I met my first proper boyfriend, a twenty-one-year-old son of a coal merchant. One evening when I finished work he asked me out. I kept hearing my grandmother's voice – 'Men only regard you as a piece of meat' – but he looked as if he might be able to offer something new and different, so I agreed to see him.

The only sort of social life I had with Lil and Tom was being taken down to the Conservative Club on a Saturday evening to sit watching the grown-ups dragging one another around the dance floor. Every so often we would all have to huddle round my grandmother to cover up the fact that she was pouring gin from a hip flask into the tonics which they bought her from the bar. Not only did the dishonesty of it all fill my religious little soul with horror, I couldn't believe the mean-spiritedness of it either.

Compared to us, my admirer was a man of considerable means

– he had central heating and a Ford Zephyr, apart from anything else. He was a big fat bloke who had the money to take me to places I had never been before, like a gambling club where he would spend the evening playing chemin de fer. I would look around at the other people with their smart clothes and sophisticated manners and yearn to escape permanently into their world instead of having to go back to Lil and Tom.

Sometimes we would get talking to someone at one of his clubs and go back to their home afterwards. The luxury of these people's lifestyles astounded me, opening my eyes to the way the middle classes lived. My partner was always a perfect gentleman, never expecting more than a chaste kiss goodnight and always getting me home on time. Lil thought he was a wonderful catch.

At one of the clubs I met a woman called Maureen who lived just round the corner from us and who was very into the local music scene. She was always going to the Trocadero in Derby to see the Liverpool groups that came touring, and would often get to meet them afterwards. She started taking me along with her and I spent evenings with people like the MoJos and the Swinging Blue Jeans. It was an exciting and glamorous life. I discovered I liked the company of musicians. It was all so different from the humdrum existence of a small provincial town.

At sixteen I realized I no longer had to put up with anything if I didn't want to. I might not be able to vote or marry without my parents' consent, but neither of those options interested me particularly anyway. What I could do was escape. I packed a small suitcase and headed off again, this time on my own. Just like thousands of other teenagers before and after me, I believed that London was waiting with open arms. All I had to do was turn up and the adventures would begin.

I found my way to High Street Kensington, where I was distracted from my search for accommodation by a display of hair bands studded with diamanté in a shop window.

'Would you like one?' a foreign man's voice asked, and I turned to see a rather overweight, swarthy, middle-aged man talking to me.

'Yes, I like them,' I said innocently.

'OK, come on.' He took me into the shop and bought me a twinkling band. When he asked me where I was going, I told him I had no plans. He invited me back to his flat in the Brompton Road. My grandmother's warnings started rattling around inside my head but he appeared to be very polite and kind. There seemed to be no reason to fear him, so I agreed to go. The flat was very neat and elegant, filled with flowers and obviously belonged to someone with money. I guessed he lived alone.

'Don't spend all your money on some cheap hotel,' he advised, 'you should try to find a flat to share.'

'Yeah,' I agreed, 'I'd like that. How do I go about it?'

He seemed to like the idea of being able to help me, going out and buying an evening paper and looking through the small ads. Looking back on it I'm sure he was gay, and just lonely for young company. When he saw a flat advertised down the road in Kempsford Gardens, he gave me the phone and suggested I make the call myself. The rent was ten and six a week, which was about what I had expected to pay for one night in a hotel.

I went round to have a look and moved in the next day, following a peaceful night on the sofa in my benefactor's flat. I kept in touch with him for a while but one evening, when he had invited me round for supper, he tried to persuade me to go out with one of his friends. The idea of having a boyfriend or a date didn't interest me at all and Black Nana's warnings about men came back like a police siren in my ears. So I refused his offer of an introduction and the atmosphere became difficult. I didn't see him any more, but by helping me with the flat he had set me on the road to a new life. Things were about to change.

3

Once I had moved to London I became Kathy, which is the name I have stuck with ever since, and I dyed my black hair red. I was someone completely new, with no connection to my family or my childhood. During the week I worked behind the counter in a chemist's in the Earl's Court Road, which gave me enough money to pay my share of the rent and buy the basics I needed. I have always loathed shopping. As long as I had clothes, food and a bit to spare I was happy. The flat was pretty tatty by today's standards but it was certainly no worse than anywhere I had lived before.

As a young, unattached girl-about-town, it was never hard to find somewhere to go on a Saturday night. So it didn't seem unusual when one of my new flatmates suggested I go with her to a birthday party somewhere between Swiss Cottage and Hampstead.

The party was already in full swing by the time we got there, a flat full of noise, young bodies and cigarette smoke, every available surface covered in cans, bottles and receptacles being used as ashtrays. It was the seventeenth birthday party of some-one called Angela, an exotic-looking girl with coffee-coloured skin, long, thick, blue-black hair and flashing eyes. I liked her immediately. She was wild and dangerous and laughed all the time.

The flat belonged to John Mayall, but the name didn't mean anything to me. Angela, however, had come with someone called Chas Chandler, a member of the Animals, a group which was then topping the charts with 'House of the Rising Sun', and them I had heard of. Chas was a giant of a man, six foot four tall with a girth to match. His hair flopped forward over his boyish face in a fashionable fringe and his accent was so thickly Geordie it was hard to tune in to what he was saying against all the background noise.

As we sat around the kitchen giggling and gossiping, Angela asked me if I lived in London.

'Yeah, I'm sharing a flat in Earl's Court.'

'God, you're so lucky,' she puckered her pretty face into a grimace, 'I'm still stuck at home with my mother in Chadwell Heath. I'd love to find somewhere in town.'

'My room-mate is just about to go back to Australia,' I said, 'you could take over from her if you like.'

Her enthusiasm was immediate and genuine and from that day to her violent death thirty years later, Angela King became my best friend.

She moved into the basement to share the back bedroom with me, adding all her clothes and records and hectic social life to the existing chaos. We spent most of our time using our flat-mates' beds in the front room as sofas where we lounged around smoking, talking and playing pop records. Every so often some-one would appear down the steps with a call for one of us on the payphone. We would dash upstairs and there would nearly always be an invitation to some party or other. This was just how I had always imagined life should be. There was no one to say 'don't' or 'can't', or to sniff disapprovingly or predict our imminent downfalls. We drank too much, smoked too much, ate unwisely and slept hardly at all. It was wonderful.

There was a basement café in the busy, cosmopolitan, scruffy

Earl's Court Road called the Chemin de Fer, which would stay open until three in the morning to cater for the beatniks and other bohemians of the area. If we had nothing else to do we would be there all night, eating corn on the cob and drinking hot chocolate, listening to the regulars arguing, philosophizing and putting the world to rights. Everyone was brimming over with ideas about how the world should be. Everyone seemed to be young and unshackled by the preconceptions and worries that I had been told were the natural accompaniment of adult life. Most of it was probably nonsense but it was funny and interesting nonsense, a million miles from the domestic trivia and constant complaining that constituted conversation back home.

Brenda, a very straight and down-to-earth girl from Devon, was the first of our group to become besotted with a man. Men usually had a hard time breaking into our circle, but there were always the persistent ones who managed to find a way past our defences. He turned out to be the manager of a strip club in Soho but even that didn't put her off. We all tried to warn her but he had her hooked and only had to reel her in. When she discovered she was pregnant we were all deeply shocked. Sex wasn't something we discussed at all: the sixties were not quite in full swing and the pill was not yet on the market. Falling pregnant was looked on as the price young girls paid for straying from the straight and narrow – yet another good reason to avoid contact with men. Brenda and the baby moved into a basement in Moscow Road where her mother was working as the housekeeper. It was a terrible warning to us all, even more effective than my grandmother's dire pronouncements. None of us wanted to share Brenda's fate, losing our freedom for a few minutes of pleasure.

I did, however, start to go out with boys, and would occasionally end up going to bed with them. I didn't take precautions because there weren't any and nobody bothered then. It was just

A rare photograph of me with Mum, Dad and my brother John

Lil and Uncle Jack on a day out

Me, aged about three

Lil, in one of her beloved caravans

The outfit the nuns made
for my confirmation

My rival, Tom, aged about twenty-two

Dad, as I found him,
after many years apart

I don't really
want to be here . . .
me, Lil and Tom

Black Nana and Lil with Tom, wigs and matching shoes

Me, on arrival in London or soon after

something people did. Sex didn't live up to any of my grand-mother's predictions of how I would be 'any man's meat'. I couldn't see what all the fuss had been about.

I was beginning to find my job at the chemist's irksome. Being on my feet in a shop all day tended to make me too tired by the evening to be able to enjoy myself. The last thing I wanted to have to do was get to bed early just so that I could get up in time to work for someone else. So I left the chemist's and took a job as an evening waitress at the Golden Egg in Leicester Square. This meant that I could sleep during the day and stay out till four in the morning, which, I had discovered, was the time when the most interesting things happened in the city.

The Golden Egg restaurants were a chain which purported to bring American cooking to Britain, although any American tourists that found their way in were sorely disappointed. The speciality was eggs with various other fried or grilled foods like chips or the great English breakfast. The best thing on the menu, in my opinion, were the pancakes with maple syrup and whipped cream.

It was hard work but I enjoyed it and the opportunity it gave me to talk to different people. I was earning thirty pounds a week there with tips, which was a lot more than any shop would pay. I knew quite a few girls who took up waitressing at that time and some of them were still doing it over twenty years later because the money was so good, particularly at the Hard Rock Café in Piccadilly.

Angela and I had a couple of highly camp gay friends living a few streets away who used to keep us amused for hours on end while posing no threat to our friendship. One evening we were on our way round to visit them when a long black limousine pulled up at the kerb beside us, honking its horn and flashing its lights. The window whistled down and inside were the

Animals, on a night out. I guess they had been to our flat looking for Angie and had been sent on to intercept us.

'We're going to a club,' one of them called out, 'do you two want to come?'

We both bundled into the car, which headed up to Great Windmill Street in the heart of Soho, just behind Piccadilly Circus. We were all intoxicated with the idea of being young, free and chauffeured around town in a limo. The car was too big to get into Ham Yard, the tiny cobblestone back alley which housed the Scene Club, so we had to climb out. The boys led us into the gloomy side street and down some steps to the club where they had done their first London gig.

The dark, smoky, underground room, big enough to hold 200 people between its black walls if they stood close enough together, was exploding with noise as we came through the door. The walls were painted black and the floor, which was covered in discarded fag ends and chewing gum, was bare of any traces of furniture. There was nothing to do but dance or stand and watch. The group up on stage was the High Numbers, and the first thing I noticed was the drummer who was going wild, crashing and pounding away like a possessed thing. He seemed to me to be the driving force of the band.

It wasn't long before the High Numbers changed their name to the Who. The drummer, of course, was Keith Moon.

After they had finished they came down to join us. Pete Townshend kept himself pretty much to himself right from the beginning, but all of the others were really friendly. Keith was always frantically exuberant, like an overgrown puppy that didn't know its own strength. He was very attractive and I really took to him, partly because he was so hyperactive and a compulsive practical joker.

Angie and I became regulars at the Scene, going down there after my shift had finished at the Golden Egg and staying until it closed in the small hours, then, when everyone had been thrown out, Keith and I used to wander around the streets of Soho, talking and joking. There were no coffee bars in those days, so there was nowhere to go once the clubs had finished except back to people's flats. The Who were signed up by Kit Lambert, who was trying to launch Track Records. He had a flat in Ivor Court at the top of Gloucester Place. One night Keith and I walked all the way up there from a gig at the Scene, talking constantly. We passed a garage called Moon's Garage and he convinced me that it belonged to his family. I was an easy target for him, gullible and innocent and willing to believe almost anything he chose to tell me.

Herman's Hermits were very big at the time, but were treated as a bit of a joke by the serious musicians in London. If they came down to the club Keith used to be incredibly cruel to them, dancing around poor Peter Noone like a puppet singing 'No milk today' in a squeaky, lispy voice while the rest of us sniggered rather shamefacedly. It was hard not to be amused by Keith, even when you didn't really approve of what he was doing.

The Hermits also had a flat in Ivor Court and Keith was unable to resist the temptation to continue taunting them at every opportunity. One night, as they drew up in the road below, he dropped a penny from Kit's window, high up in the block of flats, which made a huge dent in the roof of their van.

For a while Keith and I went to bed together but he was really too much of a loon to be a lover, more interested in getting high and playing practical jokes. He went on to have a string of brainless dolly-bird girlfriends and that left us free just to hang out together occasionally as friends and relax. It seemed to me that sex always put an extra strain on friendships unless it was kept very casual. I didn't want the sort of relationship that would exclude me from doing what I wanted and seeing whoever I wanted. I didn't have time for jealous scenes and long justifications for everything I did. I certainly wasn't looking for someone to marry and settle down with, that was exactly the sort of thing I was running away from. Most of the men I met who were starting out in the music business seemed to have the same idea – few of them wanted to get tied down into relationships which would interfere with their music or their careers. They had the same priorities as us and that suited Angie and me very well indeed.

The Scene Club was my introduction to the London rock scene, starting right at the top. Angela and I always came in with the 'stars' and were treated like royalty. We dressed as we liked and went wherever we liked without thinking for a second that we would have trouble getting in, because all the bouncers and waiters soon knew our faces. For the next five or six years clubs like the Scene were to be second homes to us, places where we ate, drank and socialized, never being asked for money, which was just as well since we seldom had enough even to buy ourselves drinks, let alone pay for entrance fees or meals. We were always being shown to the best tables, even if it meant moving other people off them. It all seemed perfectly natural to us as we went from place to place with our friends. Angie and I were unaware of just how influential the musicians were that we mixed with. Without realizing it, we had joined an élite band of people who, over the next few years, were destined to reach extraordinary heights of international fame and fortune.

We met Georgie Fame at the Scene and he took us across to the Whisky A Go Go in Wardour Street, opposite the entrance to Chinatown, where he was playing. Now we had two haunts, and over the coming months others would begin to spring up to cater for the increasing appetite for rock music. The club which later ended up being a virtual second home to us was the Speakeasy. There was a young guy who always used to sit at a table inside the door, studying the stars as they came and went.

He was noticeable because of his extraordinarily long black hair. We used to make jokes about him because he looked like a bit of a geek but none of us spoke to him or knew anything about him until years later when he became famous as Freddie Mercury.

As we couldn't afford to buy alcohol in the early days it didn't worry us that the Scene wasn't licensed. Occasionally someone would go out to the pub opposite to get drinks, but mostly we took 'purple hearts', as the fashionable amphetamines of the day were called. Everyone seemed to have them and would happily share with anyone who asked. I think they were widely available on the streets of Soho for a few pence. I never actually had to go out and score any myself.

Although Angela was a little younger than me she had been mixing in these circles a year longer and knew more about things like drugs. She often mocked me for being too 'sensible' and not as willing as she was to throw myself wholeheartedly into the unknown. I was more cautious than that, but I couldn't have managed to keep going without the purple hearts.

With their help we needed only four or five hours' sleep most nights, which allowed us to stay awake into the small hours, dancing, listening to the music and socializing to our hearts' content. It was mostly live music in the clubs, played by the people we knew, interspersed with bluebeat records.

One day Keith and I went to visit Georgie Fame. He was living with a blonde woman in a flat in a horrible tenement block in Islington. She was an artist and the walls were lined with her erotic, oriental drawings of women in the midst of sex acts with tigers and lions. Here, among the fantasies and dreams of this woman's fertile imagination, I smoked my first joint. Keith and I staggered home in a giggling daze. This was a big step into something I had never done before. The company I was keeping and the sophistication of the circles in which I was now moving made me feel that I was going in the right direction at last.

Angie and I began going to a new club, the Cromwellian, opposite the Natural History Museum in Cromwell Road. It was owned by two wrestler brothers and somehow, God knows how, I got a job as a disc jockey, starting work late at night and going on into the early morning. I played all sorts of music. The owners wanted me to play mainly dance, but later on I'd play music that I liked, such as Ray Charles, Nina Simone and Dionne Warwick, because most people just wanted to relax and talk.

One of the most respected musicians who played in the clubs was Zoot Money with his Big Roll Band. Angie and I met his wife, Ronnie Money, at the Scene and immediately fell under her spell. She was thirteen years older than me, very tiny, very pretty, and fiercely protective of us, like a sort of tough mother hen. She was from Glasgow and as hard as any Londoner, but everyone liked her. One evening we were telling her that we had to get out of the basement in Earl's Court because the landlord wanted it back so that he could sell the house.

'There's a flat above us in Gunterstone Road,' she said. 'Why don't you move in there?'

In fact it was just one room with a little kitchen, but that was fine by us. We had to share a bathroom with the Moneys, but they had a shower fitted downstairs so they hardly ever came upstairs to use it.

Andy Summers, who was playing with Zoot's Big Roll Band and who later joined the Police, was in the basement and for a few weeks Angie went downstairs to live with him, much to my annoyance. She soon came back, however, complaining that she had woken up in the night and found him under the sheets examining her with a torch.

About this time I decided that I'd had enough of the Golden Egg. I wanted to be a hairdresser and have a 'proper' job as well as the DJing, but one which didn't involve getting up too early.

I took an apprenticeship in a little salon in Kensington. Even though we didn't start till ten in the morning I still couldn't quite manage to be a good timekeeper, but I enjoyed the work all the same. Those were the days when ladies went to hairdressers and sat, covered in rollers, under domelike dryers. Hand-held dryers and trendy salons were still a thing of the future. It was a world ruled by Raymond (Mr Teasy Weasy); Vidal Sassoon was only just starting out. I wouldn't have minded making hairdressing a bit more hip but I was too distracted by my social life to put my heart into anything.

One night I was with a group of people in a pub in Wardour Street, opposite the Marquee Club, when someone introduced me to Brian Jones. He joined us and we went down to the Scene Club. By then the Rolling Stones were already big stars and Brian looked the part, already a bit of a dandy and aware of his good looks. He was a gentle, rather distant creature, with a devilish smile. He was always a loner and already felt that the other members of the band were trying to push him out, particularly Mick Jagger and Keith Richards, even though he was their founder and still looked on himself as their leader.

Over the next few months we drifted into a relationship which, like my relationship with Keith, quickly transformed into another good friendship. We started out having sex together but it was all pretty half-hearted and before long I realized that he didn't fancy me much more than I fancied him. What really turned him on, I gradually discovered, was using prostitutes. Once the girls had left, however, he used to feel lonely and would call, asking me to go over. His kitchen was always a horrible mess and I was generally unable to resist washing up the piles of dishes before doing anything else.

He often rang and asked me to go shopping with him in the King's Road. At the time he was into well-cut suits and cuban-heeled Chelsea boots which were what most mods were wearing. Although I never enjoyed shopping for myself I would let him talk me into going with him. He enjoyed being a famous face but the paranoia which would later destroy him was already showing itself and he would have sudden panic attacks when we were in shops, making me run out into the street to call a cab while he hid from imaginary enemies behind the clothes racks.

The first signs of wealth were beginning to appear in the pop world by then and Brian had bought himself a Rolls-Royce with darkened windows, which made a change from taxis and the underground. If we got peckish late at night we used to drive on to Chelsea Bridge to buy cups of tea and meat pies from the tea stall where all the bikers gathered. We would sit and eat in the Rolls, looking out at the black water beyond the lights of the shack, giggling like naughty schoolchildren.

In later years, when the drugs began to burn him up, Brian became more and more difficult to be with, and even in the early days, although he was fun, already you could see the dark side of his character making life painful for him. I went on seeing him until he died and in all those years I never remember meeting any of the other members of the Stones with him except in recording studios or at big parties, which shows how isolated and lonely he must have been.

We were still very naive about our bodies and sexuality by modern standards, and so when Angie became pregnant she didn't actually realize until she was about five months gone. Visions of Brenda trapped in her basement room flashed before our eyes. Neither of us had the faintest idea what we were supposed to do. There was no way she intended to give up her job or her clubbing to bring up a child, and there was no way I was going to try to persuade her. I don't remember who the father was but it wasn't anyone Angie intended forming a permanent relationship with.

Abortion was still illegal but some friends told us that they knew of someone to contact. We duly made the phone call and a doctor-like man arrived at the house. I let him in and directed him upstairs to our room. Ronnie and I waited downstairs. When he left he told us that things should start to happen in a few hours. He wasn't wrong. Poor Angie went into labour in our little room for about twelve hours. When we finally delivered the dead foetus we had nothing to put it in apart from a bucket. It was a shattering experience for all of us and it left poor Angie weak and sick. I remember Ronnie gave her a box of chocolates called Reward at the end of it all.

Angie was eager to put the whole thing behind her and forget it had ever happened. To show how young and stupid we were, that same night we all went to the Scotch Club in St James's. Angie was taken ill with abdominal pains and collapsed. She had developed an infection and ended up in hospital, where they grilled her relentlessly. She stuck to her story that she had miscarried naturally but it was obvious that no one at the hospital believed her.

Looking back, I can see how dangerous it all was and how easily she could have died, but when, after a few days in hospital, she was back with us, we never mentioned the incident again. We were all too deeply shocked to want to discuss it. Our lives had to go on as before, that was all that mattered, and anyway, that was why she had done it in the first place.

4

Gunterstone Road was on the way into London from Heathrow airport in the west. So when Chas Chandler got off the plane with his new discovery he dropped in to see Zoot and Ronnie Money on the way to their hotel. I was still asleep, dead to the world as they jammed together with Andy Summers. During the course of the morning Ronnie came up to find me, thinking I would enjoy what was going on. Angie and I were both completely wrecked from the night before.

'Kathy,' she tried to shake me awake, 'come downstairs and meet this guy Chas has turned up with. He looks like the wild man of Borneo.'

'What guy?' I was still bleary with sleep and wished she would just go away and leave me alone. There were always people dropping in downstairs, what could be so special about this visitor?

'He's called Jimi Hendrix, he's a guitarist Chas found working in a club in New York, and he's going to manage him. Chas says he's the best he's ever heard. Come down and meet him.'

'Later, Ronnie,' I pleaded. 'I didn't get to bed till six, let me sleep a bit longer and then I'll be down.'

'OK.' She could see that I was a lost cause and disappeared.

It was Saturday and I must have had a day off from the salon because I went straight back to sleep and didn't go downstairs until much later, by which time Jimi and Chas had disappeared to their hotel.

'Don't worry,' Ronnie assured me, 'we're all going to meet later at the Scotch.'

The Scotch Club, in Mason's Yard, off Jermyn Street in the West End, had become one of our most regular haunts. It was a lot more salubrious than the Scene, with a bar, tables and chairs and a plaid carpet. It attracted show-business people like Tony Booth, Cherie Blair's father, who was well known at the time. Things could still get very heavy and one night when I was down there a vicious fight broke out when a group of south Londoners with a grudge came in. Chairs were thrown around, bottles were broken and people's faces were cut up. I stayed under the table until it was all over, unable to get out as the doors were blocked.

That evening, when Angie, Zoot, Ronnie and I walked in, I was aware of an incredible stillness in the atmosphere. Everyone in the club was listening attentively to someone in the corner playing a guitar. People were always getting up at the Scotch and jamming but usually the club carried on around them, everyone talking and drinking. This was different; the whole place seemed mesmerized. Obviously something special was happening. It took a few moments for my eyes to adjust to the dark and I couldn't see the guitarist as I made out Chas, going up on to the stage and telling the guy he had to stop playing.

We made our way over. Chas was with his girlfriend, Lotta, Georgie Fame and his girlfriend of the time, Carmen, and another extraordinarily glamorous dark-haired girl I didn't recognize. She looked like she might be a model. As we fussed about, organizing ourselves round the table, I realized that it was Chas's new discovery who had been playing on stage, the 'wild man' Ronnie had been telling me about that morning.

'I had to get him off.' Chas was agitated as he came back.

'He's only got a seven-day visa and he's not supposed to be working, paid or unpaid.' He introduced Jimi to those of us who hadn't yet met him. I waited for Chas to say the name of the girl I didn't know, but he didn't, so I guessed she and Jimi already knew each other.

I was instantly attracted. I had never seen such an exotic man before. To my naive and unsophisticated eyes he seemed dangerous and exciting. He was dressed in slightly flared beige trousers and a white satin shirt with a large collar and wide sleeves. His hair was standing up from his head in his own version of the Afro style, another new concept in London. His voice was very seductive with his American accent, quiet and polite, his eyes attentive as he spoke. We talked generally for a while and then the glamorous girl sitting next to Jimi disappeared to the Ladies.

'Come over here,' he smiled and beckoned to me to take her seat so that we could talk more intimately. 'I want to tell you something.' I moved next to him.

'What is it?' I leant my head down to catch his voice amid all the background noise.

He kissed me on the ear and whispered, 'I think you're beautiful.'

It was a corny line but there was something so sweet and innocent about the way he said it. I liked him immediately. I felt flustered by his flattery and tried to cover it up with casual conversation.

'So what were you doing in New York?' I asked.

'I was playing in the Café Wha, that's where I met Chas.'

The dark-haired girl came back from the loo and had to sit in my old seat next to Ronnie. I didn't take much notice, assuming that she wasn't his girlfriend or he wouldn't be flirting so outrageously with me. A few minutes later Ronnie exploded into a torrent of Glaswegian abuse in response to something the girl had said to her about me. The girl grabbed Ronnie's hair and pulled her head back, which anyone who knew Ronnie could have told her was a big mistake. Ronnie picked up a bottle of whisky and smashed it down on the marble-topped table, sending splinters of glass flying in all directions and attracting all eyes in the club. Everything went horribly quiet.

'Let go of my fucking hair,' Ronnie snarled, every inch the ferocious Gorbals street fighter. She pushed the jagged end of the broken bottle up to the beautiful girl's exposed throat.

'Jesus Christ,' Chas looked panic-stricken as he turned to me, 'get Jimi out of here for God's sake, Kathy, he's only on a visitor's visa. Take him back to the Hyde Park Towers. Quick, before someone calls the police.'

'OK.' I hustled Jimi out into Mason's Yard and on to the pavement. 'Let's get a taxi,' I said, turning round just in time to see him stepping straight in front of a cab, looking the wrong way. I pulled him back as the driver screeched to a halt, opened the cab door and bundled him in.

'What was all that about?' I asked once we had calmed down enough to talk.

'I don't know.' He seemed perplexed and rather shocked at this introduction to the London social scene.

'Who was that girl?' I asked.

He shrugged and grinned a little shamefacedly. 'Nothing to do with me,' he said. 'She's Keith Richards's girlfriend. I met her in New York.'

'So that's Linda Keith.' I had heard about the beautiful model Keith Richards had been going out with but hadn't actually met her before. I could tell that Jimi had a better idea about what was going on than he was going to admit but I didn't press it. We started to get to know each other properly on the way to the hotel, where we ordered some drinks and waited for the rest of the party to join us. I couldn't quite believe how quickly I'd acquired myself a boyfriend.

Over the next hour or so everyone from our table at the Scotch Club turned up along with the rest of the Animals. They were all teasing Jimi about Linda Keith and the outburst but he continued to deny everything with an amiable grin. He was totally charming to everyone and didn't seem to have a nasty thought in his head. He was so self-effacing that nobody could have disliked him and after a few drinks he became very funny.

We talked for hours and I grew to like him more and more. He was completely different to anyone I had ever met before. Eventually he asked, 'Shall we go to my room?'

'Yes,' I said, 'all right.'

We got up and everyone said, 'Goodnight, Kathy, goodnight, Jimi,' as if we were an old married couple they had all known for years.

'What about your girlfriend?' I teased as we went upstairs.

'You're my girlfriend,' he smiled sweetly.

I was struck by how few possessions he had. Apart from his guitar there was just a small holdall with a change of clothes, a jar of Valderma for his spots and a set of rollers he used to maintain his distinctive hairstyle.

'You travel light,' I said, gesturing at the bag.

'It's all I own,' he admitted, 'look at this.' He proudly pulled out a passport and opened it up for me. 'Chas got this for me, isn't it great,' he laughed like a small delighted boy. 'We had to pay people to say that they had known me for two years because I've been moving around a lot, and we had a hell of a job finding my birth certificate.'

That night was a revelation to me. Jimi was far more sexually experienced and imaginative than any of the friends I had been to bed with. Before meeting Jimi sex had been more of a way to pass the time, an extension of adolescent messing about. He was the first man I had met who I didn't want to leave. I had never felt even a twinge of regret when my physical relationships

62

finished with men like Keith and Brian because I far preferred having them as good friends, but with Jimi there was something altogether different going on. I wanted him to be my lover as well as my friend.

The next morning I was woken by the sound of a key turning in the hotel door and Linda Keith exploded into the room before I had time to do anything. Snatching Jimi's guitar from its case she swung it up as if about to bring it down on our heads.

'Wait, wait, wait!' Jimi protested as I dived under him for protection. 'Not the guitar.'

She paused, obviously having second thoughts and turned on her heel. She stormed out, taking the instrument with her. We leapt out of bed, pulling sheets around ourselves and went to the window. Outside there was a dark blue Jaguar parked by the kerb, not the sort of car either of us were used to riding in at the time. We watched her stalk out, throw the guitar on to the back seat, climb in and drive away.

'Oh man,' Jimi moaned as if someone had just kicked him in the stomach, 'not my guitar.'

To begin with I didn't understand just how serious the situation was, but he began to tell me about all the years when he was growing up and his father wouldn't buy him a guitar, and how he had to make do with a broom handle with some strings tied to it. He told me how he had felt when he got his first guitar and how it had become like an extra limb for him. I could see that his heart was near to breaking.

'I've no money to buy a new one,' he admitted, 'and Chas don't have no extra cash. Without my guitar I might as well give up and go home.'

While we were talking the phone rang. Jimi picked it up and made a face at me to indicate that it was Linda. He listened, tried pleading a little and then just grunted agreement to her demands.

'She says I can't have the guitar back until I get rid of you,' he told me as he hung up. 'She's going to call again in twenty minutes. You'll have to go. I'll call you later.'

I could see from the panic on his face that this was not the time to argue or take a stand, so I dressed and went back to Gunterstone Road, feeling totally confused. He might be telling me that she wasn't his girlfriend, but she was certainly behaving as if she was. Was she going to lay down the law and insist that he didn't see me again? Was that going to be the last I saw of him? I couldn't believe that he was going to choose me over a beautiful woman like Linda Keith.

That afternoon he rang as promised and I was surprised at how pleased I was to hear from him. 'She's gone,' he said, 'you can come back now.'

'Did she bring the guitar back?'

'Yes.' The relief in his voice was obvious.

From then on Chas would tease us both by saying that Jimi had had to sleep with Linda to get his guitar back. Jimi would just grin and deny it. Some years later he did finally admit that he had been staying at the Hilton Hotel in New York with Linda while Keith Richards was on tour. There were rumours that it was one of Keith's guitars which she passed on to him, but Jimi said she had bought it for him, which was why she felt justified in taking it back that morning. I have since met another girl, called Carol, who says that she bought Jimi the guitar in New York just before he came to England. Now I guess we'll never know. There are so many myths and stories surrounding Jimi's short life that it is sometimes impossible to get to the truth about anything to do with him. I suppose it happens to anyone who dies young and famous and who is not there to put the record straight when other people's memories become entangled with their fantasies.

But we all have a lot to thank Linda for, because it was she who talked Chas into going to listen to Jimi play in New York in the first place. Without her he might never have come to England or had the breaks which allowed him to create such great music. Without Linda's intervention he might never have become such a huge star. The first person she took to see him was Andrew Loog Oldham, the Stones's manager, but he hadn't been interested.

Whatever Jimi said to Linda that day must have worked because she never bothered us again. She remained involved with the Rolling Stones for quite a while, starting a relationship with Brian Jones, when he was still recovering from losing Anita Pallenberg to Keith Richards.

That day I moved out of Gunterstone Road into the Hyde Park Towers Hotel and Jimi and I became a couple. We used to talk so much in those early days. He loved to tell stories about his life and I learnt everything about his childhood in Seattle; his mother, he romantically remembered, was truly beautiful. In fact, she tragically drank herself to death. We were amazed by how similar our backgrounds were.

'They passed me around as a baby from one person to another,' he said, 'and then I ended up with a good family in California, the Champs. They had this daughter, Celestine, and I really loved her. She was my sister substitute, I guess.'

I could imagine just how much that family must have meant to him. I had latched on to Angie and her mum, Mavis, in this way, desperately grateful for any affection they could spare me, and for any sense of belonging. Mavis was a big, round Anglo-Indian nurse, always happy and laughing. Angie's sister, Betty, was totally straight. There was also a brother called Aubrey who was straighter than Betty. They had all come to England from Madras after Angie's father died when she was eight. The experience had made them very close and I loved that.

'Then Al,' Jimi went on, 'my dad, turned up at the Champs

one day like a stranger and said that I had to go back with him.'
I remembered Lil turning up at the convent after four years. 'I
was so scared of him. He used to be really tough with me. Even
on the way back to Seattle, when I became too excited and
started running around, he slapped me down. I was so angry, I
shouted at him that I would tell Celestine on him. He just
laughed at me. He was like that all the time. In the end I joined
the army just to get away from my problems and Seattle and
never went back after being demobbed.

'He didn't like the fact that I wanted to play guitar, always
putting me down and telling me to get a job. If he caught me
twanging away on my broomstick with the strings, he would
snatch it from me, sending me running out of the house.

'He won't believe that I'm here in England.' Jimi thought
about this for a while and then came up with an idea. 'I'm going
to call him,' he said. 'I'll call collect to tell him I'm here, he
won't believe it.

'Hi Dad,' he said, 'I'm in England.' I could hear the voice at
the other end sounding incredulous and after a few words he
passed the phone to me. 'Tell him,' he said, 'he don't believe
me.'

'Hello.' I took the receiver cautiously. 'Mr Hendrix, it's true,
Jimi's here in England.'

'You tell my boy,' the voice crackled angrily down the line,
'to write me. I ain't paying for no collect calls!' The phone went
dead. Jimi's face just fell and I remembered what it had felt like
being in the convent when all the other girls received letters
from home, or when their families came to collect them at the
end of term and I was left behind. In that moment he looked
just like a hurt little boy.

I realized from those few words that Jimi had not been exag-
gerating his stories about his family. It was evident that he, like
me, had never had a normal, cosy family life as a child and had

been left feeling insecure and vulnerable. Chas picking him up in New York, where he had been sleeping wherever he could find a bed, and bringing him over to England made him feel that he was in charge of his own destiny for the first time in his life. At one time in New York he had been living with a prostitute he had befriended, waiting outside the room whenever she entertained clients. He had been willing to put up with anything as long as he could play his music. The guitar had been his escape from the past and I recognized how important that was.

'I had these dreams,' he once told a reporter, 'that something was gonna happen, seeing the number 1966 in my sleep, so I was just passing time till then.' Now that 1966 had arrived he was irrepressibly optimistic.

Our experiences had given us a mutual desire to find someone we could rely on, with whom we could build our own little nest away from the world. There was an instant rapport. Having somewhere to call home was all I'd ever really wanted. I wasn't looking for love. Love was a bonus. I don't think I ever thought that anybody ever really loved anybody else. That was for slushy songs and stuff like that. Both of us knew from experience that, in the end, everyone deserts you and hurts you, which meant that we each held back enough of ourselves in the relationship to keep the other interested, without realizing that was what we were doing.

We had hardly any money at all in those early months, only the little bit that Chas was able to give us, but whenever we went out for a walk Jimi always used to stuff a dollar in his shoe for emergencies.

'A dollar won't do you any good over here,' I pointed out, but he just laughed.

'It makes me feel better. When you've been penniless you never forget it. Once, when I was down in the South, I was so hungry I ate a rattlesnake. Tasted just like chicken. Didn't have anything to put in my boot then, and didn't have a guitar – had to borrow other people's whenever I could.'

He also carried a lock of my hair in his shoe, stuck in a piece of Sellotape. It stemmed from his voodoo beliefs. He thought that if he had a piece of me on him then we were in touch with each other. When he started wearing hats he transferred the dollar and my hair to the leather band inside the crown.

'It's all to do with roots,' he explained, going on to tell me quite seriously about voodoo and how people stuck needles into effigies of their enemies, something I could never imagine this quiet, gentle man ever doing. Later, when he started to use acid, his superstitions grew more psychedelic and many of his lyrics sprung from these deep-rooted beliefs. Having spent my child-hood listening to Lil and Black Nana hearing voices and finding signs in everything they saw, followed by several years rattling rosary beads and saying 'Our Father', none of Jimi's voodoo talk seemed particularly odd to me. Nothing he told me would have surprised my mother or my grandmother. He was as much of a gypsy as they were.

He opened the door for me to become myself. Jimi gave me the security I had never previously found in my family life. The paradox was that he was probably the most insecure person I had ever met. But together we made an anchor for each other even though we were both independent, scared of commitment and really too young to understand any of it.

Whenever I told him about my past he would listen intently, understanding what I was saying because he had been through so many of the same things himself. 'I'll look after you,' he would say, 'I will always look after you.' I liked hearing that. But I knew not to bank on it. And I wasn't exactly reliable myself.

The little spare money we did have we would spend on games like Risk, Monopoly, Scrabble and Twister, which we would buy at Hamleys, London's biggest toyshop. It was as if we both wanted to indulge ourselves in the sort of childhoods we had missed. Twister, where you have to put your hands and feet into different positions on a sheet on the floor until you are knotted up so much you can only collapse, used to have us helpless with laughter. When we had a bit more money Jimi bought himself a Scalextric set. We used to set it up on the lounge floor and race each other, his blue car and my red. If he thought I was winning he would cheat by 'accidentally' disconnecting the track.

In those days we had spare afternoons and he used to like to just walk around town, marvelling at the old buildings with their gargoyles, statues and ornate decorations, like a foreign tourist. He thought London was the most wonderful place he had ever seen. I showed him the sights and took him to Portobello Road and the King's Road. We bought each other pieces of jewellery and silk scarves. He liked bright colours and sumptuous textures like silks, chiffons and velvets. In some ways his tastes were more feminine than mine. He used to wear the sort of belted Burberry-style raincoat that all American travellers seem to love, which didn't go at all with the wild hair. Although Chas soon started getting him a little media coverage, he wasn't well known then. We could wander around freely and go out in a normal way without being bothered. If we attracted attention it was because of the way he dressed, not because Jimi was a famous musician.

Neither Jimi nor I had ever been skating before and Queensway ice rink was just round the corner. 'Shall we try it?' I asked Jimi one evening when we were at a loose end.

'Sure.' Jimi was always game for a new experience.

At the rink they had trouble finding a pair of boots big enough for Jimi's size eleven feet. They managed it eventually and he tucked his flares in and we set off. Within seconds of hitting the ice we were lying in an hysterical heap, weak with laughter. The other skaters just had to make their way round us as we rolled around trying to pull ourselves up on one another, only to lose our footing and come crashing down again.

By the end of the session Jimi had got reasonably good and had actually managed to let go of the side and still stay upright, but every time I let go I went straight down again. My sense of balance had not improved since my ballet lessons at the convent. By the end my ribs were aching from laughter even more than my legs and bottom were from falling over.

Jimi enjoyed himself so much that we went back several times and by the end he was pretty accomplished, whizzing round the rink, attracting everyone's stares with his hair waving in the breeze.

'Hey,' he said one day, 'Little Richard is in town. That man owes me fifty dollars from when I was touring with him. He never did pay me that money. Let's go and see him.'

We discovered that Little Richard was staying at the Rembrandt Hotel in Knightsbridge and went round to see him after a gig. We called up to the room and to my amazement the star told us to go on up. I had dressed up specially in a powder-blue dress I was very proud of, with pearl buttons and long tight sleeves. Little Richard greeted us at the door to the bedroom with wails of camp delight and wanted to know all about the dress and whether it undid all the way down. Behind him was a range of wigs on their stands and his real hair looked extraordinary.

'Come in, come in,' he ushered, flipping his wrists and shouting through a connecting door to a sitting room, 'Mama, order us a bottle of whisky.' His mother must have done as he instructed because room service appeared a few minutes later. We all sat around drinking and talking.

Jimi eventually plucked up the courage to ask for the money and Little Richard roared with laughter, wagging a well-manicured finger at him. 'You missed the bus, man, you missed the bus,' was all he had to say on the subject.

'What did he mean, you missed the bus?' I asked as we left empty-handed.

'I overslept and missed the tour bus to the next gig,' Jimi admitted, 'so he fired me. That was when I started putting a dollar in my shoe because the day I missed the bus I didn't have a single cent on me.'

As we came out of the hotel we decided to go to the Cromwellian where I had been DJing, which was just down the road. It was a chilly night and Jimi was wearing the military dress jacket which was soon to become part of his trademark. A police van came screeching to a halt beside us and seven officers leapt out, firing questions at Jimi. He replied as calmly as possible, although we were both pretty rattled.

'Do you realize that our soldiers died in that uniform?'

'What?' Jimi looked down at the jacket, suddenly understanding. 'In a Royal Veterinary Corps dress jacket?'

'Take it off!' the first policeman ordered.

I felt embarrassed and intimidated but Jimi just quietly removed the jacket. The policemen calmed down when they saw that Jimi was going to be polite whatever they said to him and began to mutter among themselves, perhaps realizing that we were harmless and that they had gone a bit over the top. I think one of the younger ones might have recognized Jimi from the few television appearances Chas was beginning to get for him.

'Well, don't let us catch you wearing it again!' he said rather sheepishly, and off they went.

As soon as they drove off Jimi slipped the jacket back on, giving a low whistle of surprised relief.

Many years later I read an interview with Little Richard in which he talked about how Jimi Hendrix came to his hotel room in London with his 'little girl', asking to borrow fifty dollars, and that he told him he must go out and earn it. It's funny how different people remember different things.

5

During his first days in England Jimi and I spent a lot of time sitting around with Chas and Lotta in the reception area of the Hyde Park Towers, in one another's rooms or in local Indian restaurants, talking about how they were going to launch Jimi's career.

When we first took him out for a curry I was worried that everything on the menu was going to be too hot for him, but he didn't bat an eyelid. Jimi, I discovered, would eat anything, absolutely anything, except tuna or marmalade or anything I cooked.

During those endless hours together Chas would lay out his plans for finding a record company and getting Jimi bookings and media coverage. There were not as many outlets for musicians then as there are today, none of the video channels or daytime television programmes that need endless new products to fill their time slots, and only a handful of music papers, such as *Melody Maker* and *NME*.

There was much discussion about how they would form a band and what material they would play. Although there seemed to be so much to do Chas was never daunted, even though initially most of the hard work fell on his shoulders. Before anything else there were all the formalities to be sorted out, like getting Jimi a proper work permit. Till he could be sure he could stay in the country there wasn't much point making plans for promoting him and getting the right people to hear him.

The problems wouldn't end once a group was formed, either. There would be the need for instruments and equipment, which would have to be begged or borrowed, and venues to be found that were willing to book a new and unknown talent who looked like nothing they had ever seen before. He told the club owners that they would be pleased with the new act because they weren't too loud and there were only three of them, so they were cheap as well!

It all felt like a desperate race against time. If things took too long Chas would run out of money and the Immigration Department might send Jimi back to America. It seemed an impossible task to launch somebody that quickly without some serious financial backing.

None of us had any doubts that Jimi was going to be a star. We all knew, including him, that his playing was better and more original than anyone else around; it was just a question of how best to organize his rise to stardom. There was a buzz of excitement in the air as we huddled together, plotting and scheming, sitting around kicking ideas back and forth, willing to try virtually anything.

Chas took us along to watch Eric Clapton and Cream playing one of their first concerts at the London Polytechnic. It was in a room like a school hall, packed with students standing shoulder to shoulder listening as politely and attentively as any jazz club crowd. We were standing in the audience to the left of the stage and during one of the breaks between numbers Chas went up on-stage. Chas towered over everyone else and so was able to attract Eric's attention. He asked if Jimi could play with them. Ginger Baker objected, not wanting to share the glory with an unknown, but Eric agreed and somehow managed to appease Ginger.

Eric offered Jimi his guitar but Jimi declined, saying he had brought his own, which I was carrying for some reason. He took it from me and climbed on-stage. A few moments were spent messing around changing over plugs and then he went into 'Killing Floor', a standard blues. Chas had gone to the back of the stage and was standing with Eric.

At that time Jimi's playing was perfect because he was so fresh, so eager to prove himself, and totally sober. All the students in the audience were stunned by what they heard. I've read Jeff Beck being quoted as saying that he thought of throwing in the towel the first time he heard Jimi play. He was simply the best rock guitarist in the world.

'Eric nearly fainted,' Chas told us later. 'He said, "Give us a cigarette, man! Is he really this good, or can he just do the one piece?" When I told him Jimi was for real he just said, "Oh my God!"' That night we all went home feeling pretty smug.

Not long afterwards we met Eric in a club and he invited us back to his flat in Park Road, near Regent's Park – quite close to Ivor Court, where he was living with his black girlfriend, Brandy. The four of us sat around making polite conversation. Eric and Jimi hardly knew each other and were making an effort but it was very stilted. They both wanted to be friendly but Eric was well known for not having the gift of the gab and Jimi could be a reticent character.

'God,' Jimi muttered as we came out, 'that was hard work.'

Chas had a lot of ideas about stage clothes, wanting Jimi to wear the sort of blue mohair suits with smart little collars that all the other groups were wearing then. Jimi would politely go along with whatever Chas said, but once we were alone he would raise his eyes to the sky.

'I hate mohair suits,' he would wail. 'I had enough of wearing those stupid suits when I was on the Chit'lin' Circuit with people like Little Richard and Ike and Tina Turner, doing all those dumb dance steps. I hated doing all those dinky little dances!'

Once we were all standing in the reception area at the hotel and I was wearing a Biba trouser suit topped by a little beret with a bobble on top. It was a fitted jacket with a Nehru-type collar. I was always pretty conservative in my tastes compared to the people I hung around with.

'You should wear suits,' Chas was saying to Jimi for the millionth time, 'a bit like the one Kathy's wearing.' For a moment Jimi looked as if he was about to choke but he managed to turn it into a grunt of semi-agreement, muttering that it 'looked OK on a girl' and hoping that Chas would get the message. But Chas didn't. He had set his heart on producing a clean-cut image in the style of the other groups of the time.

At this point, however strongly he objected Jimi never openly argued. He realized that Chas knew more about the British rock scene than he did and was working hard to get his career going. He respected his opinion. But it wasn't long before he stopped being so willing to do as Chas asked. All the time he listened to Chas's ideas he knew that sooner or later he would be able to do his own thing and wear the sort of clothes he liked, which were the things he wore every day. Jimi knew exactly what image he wanted, but he had to wait until the moment was right before he could do anything about it. He allowed Chas to believe he was going along with his ideas, but if there was one thing Jimi hated, it was being told what to do, whether it was by a manager, an audience or a girlfriend, and if he was forced into an option he tended to do the opposite. As he became more successful this character trait grew to be more of a problem.

Chas wanted to get into management because the Animals had broken up by then, but he didn't have the money needed to launch an act quickly. Pop groups did not make huge sums at that time unless they wrote their own material, and the Animals had run into considerable financial problems. Even in those pre-video days it was expensive to launch a new act. You needed to be able to hire studios and backing musicians and you needed to pay the act enough to live on while you waited for the deals to come and the money to roll in. Even our modest daily expenses were becoming more than Chas could afford.

People have said that he sold a guitar to keep Jimi in those early weeks, but I have no memory of that. I do, however, remember Chas coming to our room with the hotel bill, complaining that because I was there they were now charging a double-room rate and he didn't have the money to pay for it. We went down together to see the manager and confessed that we couldn't pay that much. He very kindly changed it back to a single-room rate without any argument.

Whatever the exact sums may have been we certainly needed some outside finance, so Chas brought in Mike Jeffery, who was the Animals' manager, to help with the money and contacts. (His real name was Mike Jeffery, but for some reason we always called him Mike Jefferies.)

Mike came round to the hotel and both Jimi and I liked him. He was very different to all the other people we knew: older, better educated, slicker and more businesslike. He had started his career running a jazz club on behalf of the Newcastle University Students' Union which was how he had met the Animals. To Jimi and me he seemed like someone we could look to for guidance, someone we could trust.

Each day at the hotel started for us at about lunchtime when we would have tea and toast in bed, which the management brought up to us on red napkins. We always slept through the mornings because we would stay out all night at the clubs, listening to music and meeting the people who were making it. Everyone in the business had heard about Jimi within a few weeks and they all wanted to hear him play.

The other member of our inner circle was Chas's girlfriend, Lotta. Chas was a typical northern working-class man of the time, who thought that a woman's place was under her man's thumb. Lotta fitted his needs perfectly. She was Scandinavian and totally subservient. She did everything Chas told her with absolutely no argument or initiative of her own, and in return he was very protective of her. We were all so broke that at one stage Lotta had to take a job as a hat-check girl at the Bag O' Nails which was owned by two guys called the Gunnells. They were a couple of hard men from somewhere in south London. The Gunnells had been in a feud with some other family and there were rumours that the club was going to be petrol-bombed. When Chas heard about this he panicked and Lotta had to leave straight away.

Though Chas was a very strong character and everyone had words with him at one time or another, he was loved for his plain speaking. Even at his funeral someone stood up and said, 'There isn't anyone in this church who hasn't had a run-in with Chas at some time in his life.' In those days Lotta was the exception, and it was only much later that she did finally assert her independence from him.

Bit by bit I moved my stuff out of Gunterstone Road and into the hotel. Within a couple of weeks I told Ronnie that I didn't need the flat any more and it was let to someone else. By that time Angie had moved in with Eric Burdon, the lead singer of the Animals, in Duke Street, St James's where he was renting a flat from the manager of the Scotch Club.

Mike Jeffery was confident that he had the contacts necessary to get Jimi his work permit, but there was still a lot of worry when Jimi got his first booking as support band to Johnny Halliday who at that time was France's biggest star by far. Chas and Mike were afraid that if Jimi went to France the British authorities might not let him back into the country. Johnny Halliday had heard Jimi play at Le Kilt Club in Frith Street. Le Kilt was another of Louie Brown's clubs like the Scotch. The main differences were that the carpet was a different tartan and the place was full of young French people. (I was sitting next to Halliday on the night he was there but had no idea who he was.) He had asked if Jimi would be able to get a band together in time to play with him. Mike sorted out the official paperwork just in time and the booking was confirmed. Jimi was very excited about the gig, even though neither of us had ever heard of Johnny Halliday. At that stage he was up for anything; if you had told him there was an amp up on the common he would have been out there playing. It was all he lived for.

His excitement faded a little when Chas turned up at the hotel with a blue suit for him to wear, just as he had been threatening to do. Since Jimi had been nodding and agreeing to everything, and because it had obviously cost Chas more money than he could afford, he couldn't very well get out of wearing it this time. I actually thought he looked really nice in it.

A more pressing problem than what to wear, however, was who to hire as backing musicians. Whenever Jimi played in the clubs he just jammed with whoever was around. He didn't have anyone he played with on a regular basis. This, however, was a serious concert tour and we had to find a band.

'They don't have to be brilliant,' Chas said, 'because Jimi can carry them with his playing. They just need to be proficient enough to keep up with him.'

He needed a drummer and a bass guitarist and auditions were held in a small, seedy basement club in Soho with black walls and coloured graffiti. Chas and Jimi were judging musical ability and asked Lotta and me if we thought they looked right. They wanted the act to look sexy and fit in with Jimi's image as well as play well. The first drummer's name was Aynsley Dunbar and the guitarist was Noel Redding. Noel Redding had previously auditioned for the Animals. He was really a rhythm guitarist but was able to play a good bassline which was what they were looking for, and he looked the part. Chas immediately gave him the job. Noel was an ordinary young man from Folkestone with no airs and graces. He just wanted to play guitar and get paid for it. Aynsley had played with the Mojos – we had met in the North before I came down to London. He was very good and they were quite prepared to offer him the job. Then Mitch Mitchell, who had just left Georgie Fame's Blue Flames, auditioned the following week and they were completely unable to choose between Mitch and Aynsley. Chas told Mitch he would let him know and we all climbed into a taxi to go back to the hotel. Chas and Jimi debated the pros and cons of the two drummers but they couldn't make up their minds.

'Let's toss for it,' Chas said eventually, when it was obvious they couldn't make a choice any other way. He pulled a coin out and flipped it. Mitch Mitchell became Jimi Hendrix's new drummer.

Mitch was completely different to Noel. He had been a child actor and was one of the Ovalteenies (a group of children used to advertise a hot drink which was fashionable in England at the time), as well as a schoolboy in a number of Terry Thomas films. As a result he had developed a stagy sort of pukka accent which at the time we all assumed was genuine, none of us having had any first-hand experience of the upper classes.

In later years many fans believed that Mitch was the perfect drummer for Jimi because he was so innovative. These innovations, however, sometimes got on Jimi's nerves and he would end up banging his guitar on the cymbals to tell Mitch he had finished playing and he could stop drumming. Even in the early days Jimi would become infuriated with Mitch's patronizing attitude, which led to him sometimes not even turning up for rehearsals. At one stage there was talk of sacking him and taking on Aynsley instead, but it was decided to give him another chance and somehow they just kept going.

After that Noel and Mitch would join us for our gatherings at the hotel, laying plans and discussing what material they would use for the imminent French gigs with Johnny Halliday. Chas was working flat out trying to get them bookings and organize record deals, but there wasn't much the rest of us could do except sit and wait for things to get started. Kit Lambert was keen to sign Jimi up for Track, his independent record company, but he needed to convince Polydor to back him and distribute the records and they didn't think Jimi was commercial enough. Chas really wanted to get Jimi signed by Decca, but the A&R man there told him he didn't think Jimi had anything. Chas just laughed about it, saying that it was Decca's loss and reminding us that they were the people who had turned down the Beatles.

The general feeling among the big record companies was that there wasn't an opening for a guitarist who looked as way-out as Jimi. Most of the big groups like Herman's Hermits and the Dave Clark Five had clean-cut images which everyone wanted to emulate. Jimi didn't fit in with anything that was happening in the charts at the time. Chas's spirits never seemed to flag, no matter how many rejections he received. Kit Lambert had faith in Jimi because he mixed with the real musicians in the clubs and knew what they were all saying about Jimi's playing.

Jimi, Chas, Noel and Mitch had to go to France for the Johnny Halliday gigs without Lotta and me. Although there was now a little money coming from Mike Jeffery, there wasn't enough in the kitty for extra tickets. The days when Jimi could afford to support hundreds of hangers-on still hadn't arrived, and the boys had to travel to the gigs in a tatty old bus, watching Halliday purr up in a large American car.

Whenever anything happened in England, however, like going to see a record company, we all used to travel as a group.

Chas would announce that we had to go to see somebody at a certain time and off we would all trot.

After France, where Jimi had gone down politely with the Johnny Halliday fans, Chas had arranged a series of gigs at the Big Apple in Munich. At one of these one of the fans was supposed to have pulled him off-stage and his precious guitar had been damaged, and he became so angry that he started smashing up everything on-stage including his guitar. I knew nothing of this; as far as I knew he only had the one, precious, white Strat he'd brought with him from the States, and it was in perfect condition when I saw it. The greatest impression of Germany that Jimi brought back was his first sight of a duvet, which he thought was a great invention.

Then things really began to move. Chas took the Experience into the studio to record 'Hey Joe', the first single, just two months after Jimi set foot in England. We all went down together to Kingsway Studios, near the Strand, in a taxi. The studio itself was tiny and cramped. Jimi was very nervous at the prospect of singing. He had all the confidence in the world about his guitar-playing, but he had no faith in his voice. Chas was continually having to gee him along and tell him that it was easy and anyone could do it. I had to sit in the studio itself because the console area was too small to accommodate anyone surplus to essential requirements.

'Keep an eye open for the Breakaways,' Chas told me, 'they're doing the backing vocals.'

'What do they look like?' I asked, imagining them as glitzy showgirls, all made-up for the occasion.

Chas laughed. 'You'll think they're the cleaning ladies,' he said. 'They don't dress up for recording sessions.'

When they did turn up, complete with scarves over their hair, I could see what he meant. So much for the glamour of the music industry. They didn't have any chance to rehearse as every extra hour in the studio was costing Chas money, so he wrote the words on pieces of paper and held them up behind the glass for the girls to read as they sang. I was very impressed by their professionalism.

During a pause for discussion I slipped out to the loo. When I got back there was a red light on above the studio door, which meant nothing to me. Ignoring it, I pushed my way back in, making a loud clatter, and ruined the whole recording.

Chas went absolutely ape, screaming and shouting at me as I cowered in the corner, shaking and wishing I could just disappear. Some of the music-history books say that Jimi was upset at the session because Chas was shouting at him, but it was me he was yelling at, not Jimi.

I was desperately keen for Jimi to be a success because if he wasn't I knew he would have to go back to America and that would probably be the end of our relationship. I was sure that he had the potential to be a big star: he just had to get the breaks to make it happen. Chas's excitement and optimism wore off on all of us, but there were always those moments of doubt when we wondered if the breakthrough would come in time.

The record was released before Christmas, with Jimi's own composition, 'Stone Free', on the flip side (Chas had pointed out the considerable financial advantages of his recording his own material). An article about Jimi appeared in the *Record Mirror* and within weeks the single had sold 100,000 copies and was at number six in the charts. We began to hear it on the radio and in the clubs wherever we went. All Chas's predictions were coming true. Polydor were suddenly impressed and helped Kit Lambert and his partner, Chris Stamp, set up Track Records.

From then on Chas encouraged Jimi to do all his own writing, not only because it meant more money but also because he believed Jimi had real talent which he wanted him to pursue. I think Jimi's songwriting abilities had come as a pleasant surprise to Chas. He had known he had a great guitarist on his hands, but the lyrics were a welcome bonus.

Jimi was always jotting down ideas on bits of paper, strumming on his guitar as he did so. When we were together he would often spend ages sitting on the bed with the guitar, sometimes with amplifiers and sometimes unplugged so that only he could hear the sound.

'I wish you could play bass,' he said wistfully one day, 'that would be a help.'

'Are you kidding? I can't play guitar,' I protested.

'I'll teach you,' he insisted. 'It's not hard, you just have to put your fingers like this and strum like that.'

He tried for about twenty minutes to show me what to do but eventually had to accept that I was a lost cause, totally unable to master it at all. I couldn't even remember a simple chord. He tried many times to get me to get a basic bassline.

'It's easy,' he kept saying, 'just put your fingers here,' but I could never hit the right notes. He was very patient but realized in the end that I was one of those people who couldn't be taught. It became a standard joke that if we were clapping along to a song I would be clapping on the half beat when everyone else was on the beat. Perhaps he should have auditioned more carefully for musical ability when he was looking for a girlfriend! As it was, he just had someone to restring his guitars.

Jimi and Chas would talk for hours about what he was doing musically. Jimi didn't need any encouragement to create his own material. The only covers he wanted to do were of songs by people he really admired like Bob Dylan or a few blues numbers. At the beginning, before the group had a repertoire of their own, they had to do things which all of them knew, like 'Land of a Thousand Dances', so they worked hard to gather enough material for a show. They never rehearsed much as a group but seemed to manage perfectly well when they were on-stage together.

In December we moved out of the Hyde Park Towers. The hotel had been having problems with dry rot. The first we knew of it was when one of our bed legs went through the floorboards as I jumped on the bed. The management more or less evacuated us and closed down that part of the building, moving us to another floor at the back. As more and more rooms became dangerous and uninhabitable we had the place almost to ourselves, so the fact that the bathrooms had to be shared with other people didn't matter much. Most of the time it was like living in a rather large and run-down private house. One day one of the staircases fell down and another section of the hotel was blocked off. Eventually the whole place had to be closed and spent years cloaked in scaffolding being slowly rebuilt, but we were already out by that time.

We still didn't have a great deal of money. Chas must have mentioned to Ringo Starr that we were having to live in hotels and couldn't afford it because he offered us a flat he owned in Montagu Square, W1. He had moved to the country and didn't need it any more.

It consisted of the ground and lower-ground floors of a converted town house in a smart square near Marble Arch. Chas and Lotta had a white-carpeted bedroom on the ground floor, opposite the sitting room, while Jimi and I were downstairs in a room opposite the kitchen. Upstairs had an en suite bathroom with a pink sunken bath, which seemed very exotic to us, and Jimi and I had a bathroom with doors off the kitchen, and a dressing room. Our bedroom had a horrible old fireplace at one end and a lot of panelling on the walls but it was still the best place I had ever lived in and seemed a fitting home for a rising pop star. We had to share the kitchen with Chas and Lotta but we were hardly ever in there at the same time.

It was a wonderful first Christmas together. Rituals like Christmas and birthdays didn't mean much to Jimi or me, perhaps because we hadn't known much about them as children. Although we gave each other presents they were hardly ever linked to special occasions and I don't think we ever bought a tree or decorations ourselves. Chas, however, celebrated his birthday in the flat with a big party which got a bit out of hand and the Christmas tree he had bought fell on top of Bill Wyman and his girlfriend who were sitting on the floor beneath it.

We didn't have sophisticated music systems then, just a record player in a wooden cabinet along one wall of the sitting room, which we stacked records on to. Jimi mainly used it for playing the blues numbers he would buy whenever he had any spare money, from artists like Elmore James, Muddy Waters and Lightnin' Hopkins. Most of the little money he received he spent on clothes and taxi fares. We used to tour all the boutiques which were opening in Carnaby Street and the King's Road, just as I had done with Brian, although by now there was far more choice.

As the money came in we bought more records. Jimi's favourite LP was *I Started Out as a Child* by Bill Cosby. He had several of Cosby's albums which he used to play to anyone who would listen. He was a good mimic and could do the voice when he was in the mood. He used to take off David Frost as well.

We built up a large record collection during our time together, which have now been sold to Paul Allen, the Microsoft co-founder and fan who is creating the Experience Music Project in Seattle. A lot of them were bought at One Stop Records on South Molton Street. There were the old blues records which he used to listen to religiously and play along with. We also collected a mixture of other stuff, much of it given to us by musicians. Jimi also bought classical pieces like *The Planets Suite* and the *Messiah* and often he would buy on impulse, just because he saw it on the racks and wanted to find out more about it. I think he bought *The Planets Suite* because he liked the cover with its picture of the solar system and had recently been reading some science fiction. He found he quite liked it and played it a few times. Sometimes he would bring records home, play them once and never listen to them again. When John and Yoko brought our their controversial *Virgins* album, we had to have it wrapped with brown paper in the shop because of the nudes on the cover. It was considered obscene at the time and the shop assistants insisted on covering it up before we could take it out.

Living together as two couples had its problems because Jimi and I tended to have very loud rows, whereas Lotta never raised her voice or argued with Chas at all. They complained they were able to hear us going at one another from their room upstairs. Jimi was difficult to deal with, as, more than anyone, Chas was to find out. He always did whatever he wanted, regardless of how it might affect other people, and when he wanted something he wanted it immediately, whether it was possible or not.

He was particularly frustrated by the lack of decent food in England at that time. We had been brought up at the tail end of rationing and wartime shortages and British standards of catering left a lot to be desired. New Yorkers thought nothing of wandering out in the middle of the night and having a range of different restaurants and takeaways to choose from. London was still a long way behind. On top of that, my cooking skills and interest in food were virtually nil and a cause of many of our disagreements.

'Goddamnit! Why can't you learn to cook?' Jimi would rage as something indigestible appeared before him.

'Why don't you cook it yourself?' would be the general tone of my response, although the language might vary. It never occurred to me to do anything I didn't want to, just because

Jimi told me to. We were very alike in that respect and the only way forward in these situations was confrontation.

Having rows never worried either of us much; I guess we had both listened to enough of them throughout our childhoods not to take them too seriously. We could be shouting and screaming one moment and forgetting about the whole thing the next, but Chas and Lotta found this increasingly difficult to cope with. Years later Mike Jeffery's personal assistant was interviewed for a book and said that I was the only person who would stand up to Jimi. It never occurred to me to do anything else.

Chas became so disturbed by our apparently stormy relationship that eventually he and Mike Jeffery called Jimi up to Mike's management office in Gerrard Street and suggested that if we didn't stop rowing I was going to have to move out. They put it to him that we should split up anyway because they thought I was interfering with his creativity. Jimi might have been willing to keep his mouth shut about wearing mohair suits, and be advised on what material to perform, but he wasn't about to be told what to do in his private life. He told them to mind their own business.

Chas tried another tack, taking me to one side in the sitting room at home and asking whether I didn't think it would be better for us to go our separate ways. I was somewhat taken aback, having thought that our relationship was going rather well. Chas told me he was worried that we might start rowing in public and that that would damage Jimi's image. He didn't think a black singer at that time could risk behaving badly. He was always aware that Jimi might get thrown out of the country if he drew too much adverse publicity.

'No,' I said, 'I think we're all right really.'

'But Lotta and I don't row like that,' he said, apparently genuinely puzzled.

Since I had never heard Lotta even raise her voice that didn't surprise me, although some years later, after they married, she actually left Chas and went off with someone else, so perhaps it would have been better if they had had a few arguments to clear the air in the early days of their relationship.

Some of the rows between Jimi and me were quite dramatic, mainly because both of us operated on very short fuses and neither of us was ever willing to climb down, so we could only end them by one or other of us storming off – usually me. Once he was moaning about my cooking again and I felt I had put a lot of effort into whatever it was – mashed potatoes, probably. I didn't take kindly to being told they were disgusting, so I picked up the plate and smashed it on to the floor.

'Hell – what are you doing?' he screamed at me, so I picked up a few more plates and threw them around the room as well, yelling back at him. Eventually I turned on my heel and stalked out, crossing the street to find a cab. He followed, trying to persuade me to come back, but I refused to listen. I found a taxi and jumped in, and without letting Jimi hear told the driver to take me to Angie and Eric's place in Jermyn Street. When I returned the next day, having cooled down, I asked him what he had done while I was away.

'I wrote a song,' he said and handed me a piece of paper with 'The Wind Cries Mary' written on it. Mary is my middle name, and the one he would use when he wanted to annoy me. I took the song and read it through. It was about the row we had just had, but I didn't feel the least bit appeased.

On another occasion I stormed into the bathroom in preparation for a walk-out and he locked both doors from the outside. 'Let me out!' I shrieked, pounding my fists on the door.

'Have a bath,' he told me and went outside for some fresh air. Several hours later Lotta heard my cries and came to my rescue.

In various different rages I used to throw his clothes in the air and sometimes even stamp on his guitars, which was guaranteed to make him mad. I put my foot right through the back of one of his acoustic guitars. I think that was one of the things that worried Chas. He was frightened we might do some damage to Ringo's flat. We did in fact break one of the sitting-room doors by slamming it too hard. I thought Chas was going to kill us when he found out.

Once when I stormed out Jimi chased me into the street and grabbed at my skirt to pull me back. It was a pink wraparound skirt which came straight off in his hand, leaving me standing in stockings and suspenders (tights having only just been introduced).

'Coming back now?' he enquired, triumphantly, and I didn't have much choice, partly because I was laughing too much to see where I was going.

Most of the time during these spats I was threatening to go and he was trying to stop me from leaving. Once a photographer turned up in the middle of a disagreement and I was able to sneak away while Jimi stood, posing and scowling on the doorstep of the house. I've seen the resulting pictures in a number of books and Jimi looks incredibly moody as he glowers after me, unable to vent his anger or stop me without being rude to the photographer and unprofessional.

I couldn't really blame Jimi for complaining about my cooking, it was pretty basic. I remember one Christmas Day I did him egg and chips for dinner because there was no way I was even going to attempt a roast turkey or whatever else might be traditional and there were no restaurants in those days that didn't have to be booked months in advance. He was very good about it, glad to get anything to eat at all, I guess.

The media was starting to request interviews with Jimi regularly by the time we got to Montagu Square, which meant that I had to be kept hidden, since a steady girlfriend would have damaged his sexy image. Jimi was briefed never to mention me and I would stay downstairs, usually in the bath, while he entertained the journalists above. It didn't bother me, I knew it was the way things were done.

Chas and Mike were trying to promote him as a sex symbol, an idea which made him very embarrassed if they discussed it in front of him since he wasn't someone who was comfortable strutting around like a peacock. He wanted to be much cooler, although his clothes made him seem flamboyant and his highly charged sexuality was obvious to anyone who met him. Right from the beginning he had a style of his own, wearing satin shirts with voluminous sleeves, army jackets and bell-bottoms with scarves tied around the legs long before anyone else. Even Brian Jones was still wearing suits when Jimi first arrived in London and it was only later that other musicians started wearing flowery clothes, feather boas and jewellery.

Jimi was an original in his style. One of the first presents I bought him was a black shirt with roses on it which he wore all the time. It was very unusual then for men to wear anything so flamboyant. I remember finding it in a shop around Portobello Road. Jimi loved it.

6

Before 'Hey Joe' came out and became a hit, Chas had booked Jimi to do a tour of working-men's clubs in the north of England. He tried to get Jimi out of it once it was obvious that he could pull bigger crowds in other venues, but the contracts were watertight and there was nothing we could do, so he had to honour them. Jimi wasn't too bothered, happy to play anywhere if there was an audience.

We had a roadie called Gerry Stickells, who had been brought in by Noel Redding because he was good with engines and had an old van to put all the equipment in. Gerry was a big cuddly bear of a man, who has since gone on to be successful staging major rock tours around the world. Now he runs fleets of pantechnicons, but then he could get everything into the back of one beaten-up blue van. He became an integral part of our lives and a friend who helped us in innumerable ways in the coming years. You grow to know people well when you spend a few weeks together on the bench seat of a van. Mitch had a car and sometimes used to take Noel around to the gigs while Jimi travelled with Gerry in the van, with me sandwiched between them.

Jimi certainly couldn't afford a car at that stage – besides, he hadn't got a driving licence. He later discovered that he was an appalling driver, probably due to his eyesight as much as anything. On the odd occasion when he drove in America, where he didn't have to worry about handling a gearstick, he would borrow Noel's glasses and drive with his nose pressed up against the windscreen in an attempt to see the road ahead. It was a terrifying experience. He was too idle to get glasses for himself.

We always had the radio on when we were travelling since we had to have music wherever we went, usually tuned in to one or other of the pirate stations that were the precursors of Radio One, broadcasting illegally from little fishing boats off the coast.

It was while we were motoring north one dark day, with me squeezed between Jimi and Gerry as usual, with my feet on the dashboard, that 'Wild Thing' by the Troggs came on. Jimi immediately turned it up just as the old van leapt over a hump-back bridge and all the gear in the back crashed up and down.

'Wow!' he laughed, 'who's this?'

'The Troggs,' Gerry told him.

'Troggs?' Jimi looked puzzled. 'What kind of name is that?'

'Oh, they're a sort of little people,' I tried to think of a decent explanation, 'who live in the garden.'

'What,' he said, 'you English people are really funny. You think little people live in gardens?'

'Well,' I said defensively, 'you believe you can stick pins in dolls or effigies of people you don't like.'

As soon as we got back to London he bought a copy and played it to himself a few times, deciding to make a cover version which he could use in the stage show.

Chas didn't go to every booking with us and I suspect that when he did he went on the train. It was a shrewd move as the van wasn't terribly reliable and more than once Jimi and I ended up pushing it in the snow, both in our flimsy clothes and me in strappy, fashionable shoes, as Gerry tried to coax it into life. My feet were always cold in those days but I would never have considered buying a sensible pair of shoes.

On one occasion Chas did come with us, when we were playing near his home town of Newcastle. 'To save money,' he said, 'we'll skip the hotel and stay with my mum and dad.' He took us to a tiny, back-to-back tenement house which didn't even have running water. 'You guys can't sleep together here, Kathy,' he warned me. 'You and Lotta will have to share and I'll go in with Jimi.'

I think Lotta must have imagined I was going to rape her because she climbed into bed with all her clothes on, although, of course, it might just have been because of the cold. Chas sternly made us vow never to tell anyone that he had slept with Jimi Hendrix. 'Of course not,' we promised.

The punters in the men's clubs we played were far more interested in their own social life and drinking beer than listening to a bunch of young hippies. These were not the same respectful audiences that Jimi was used to in the clubs of New York and London, which were full of fellow musicians and music critics. No one here realized that they were in the presence of the greatest rock guitar talent of Jimi's generation, nor would they have cared if they had. One or two of the clubs were all beer and sawdust, brightly lit with Formica-topped tables and chairs that could be stacked together. The atmosphere was always thick with smoke and the men would sit yelling at each other over the tables with their sleeves rolled up. Some of them even wore flat caps. Jimi would ask them to pipe down while he played, which might quieten them down a little. He would turn the volume up to try to get their attention until the club managers interfered and got him to turn it back down.

He always wanted to play louder than the equipment could possibly stand, and would finish by blowing it up. This would drive Chas and Mike mad as they had to find more. I think they were being paid about twenty pounds a night, which Chas or Gerry would pick up at the end of the evening, and which would barely cover our expenses. It was weird that Jimi had actually had a hit record and the money still hadn't filtered through. We had just enough to exist on and a nice place to live when we were in London, but nothing more. It didn't matter, the breaks were coming – the people who knew about music now knew about Jimi. Fame and fortune were beginning to look inevitable but the daily grind of touring was hard work and a little spare cash would have made things a hell of a lot easier.

Once we arrived in a new town we would have to find ourselves a hotel, as it would not be pre-booked or arranged on our behalf. In Nottingham we ended up in a dowdy old inn called the Blackboy Hotel, which Jimi couldn't believe.

'I ain't staying no place called the Blackboy,' he protested, but there was no choice. He didn't really care. He thought it was quite amusing. 'Where do you English get these names from? You couldn't call a hotel the Blackboy in the States!'

If his appearance had attracted curious glances in London, he looked totally outrageous up north. Up there they might have heard about Carnaby Street and the King's Road, and seen pictures of the fashions on television, but the clothes certainly hadn't reached the average high street. Men still had short back and sides haircuts and grey-brown clothes just like their fathers before them. Wherever we went we would hear low mutters like, 'Is that a girl or what?' none of which bothered Jimi at all. As long as they didn't become threatening, he enjoyed outraging people. Quite a few thought he was gay because of his appearance (although 'gayness' was still an unheard-of concept in all but the most sophisticated corners of the country), and the words 'pansy' and 'queer' could be heard here and there. Jimi probably didn't know what they meant, and if he did he certainly wasn't offended, being more confident of his sexuality than any man I had ever met.

Chas, with all the sensitivity of a northern working-class boy who had grown up in the fifties, wasn't always as patient. One night in London he snapped. There were two Glaswegian guys giving Jimi a hard time in a pub down a small side street off Tottenham Court Road, where we had stopped for a drink on the way to the Hundred Club in Oxford Street. I think we were going to see Brian Auger or John Mayall.

'Are yer a man or a girl?' they taunted, one of them prodding him with his finger and tugging at his hair. We tried to ignore them in the hope that they would get bored and give up but it didn't work. The last thing Jimi needed at that stage was to get into a pub brawl which might end up in the press.

'Come on,' Chas said, draining his glass, 'let's drink up and go.'

We followed his example and went out into the street, but the two drunks followed us. As we walked away one of them came after us along the road, still shouting taunts, while his friend hung back a bit. I guess they thought they were in for a diverting evening of queer-bashing.

'Yer fuckin' chicken,' he yelled, 'why doncha stick up fer yerself? Are yer a fuckin' pansy then?'

'Just walk on ahead,' Chas muttered to me. He turned sharply and went back to the man, pushing his face close. 'Fuck off man, before I lay yer out.'

We couldn't resist turning back to see what was happening. The man poked Chas with his finger, an unwise thing for a drunk to do to a six-foot-three Newcastle ex-docker. Chas took a step back and then swung his leg up, kicking the man hard, bringing him down on to the pavement in one movement. He continued to kick him with startling speed and ferocity as the other drunk hurried back into the pub. Chas kept kicking until the man wouldn't be getting up for a while.

'Goddamnit,' Jimi breathed as we hurried away towards Oxford Street, 'remind me not to mess with Chas.'

All evening Jimi was unable to get over what he'd seen, stunned by the sight of his giant protector at work. It was demonstrations of support and friendship like that which made Jimi willing to take more interference in his work from Chas than from anyone else. He knew that Chas truly had his best interests at heart. Their relationship lasted longer than any other Jimi had with a male friend.

If Jimi hated the food in London, the stuff he was served up in roadside cafés and cheap northern hotels blew his mind. Luckily he liked fish and chips, so we survived mostly on that but he was constantly complaining that he was losing weight.

'Why does it have to be chips with everything?' he would moan.

Food may never have been a major part of my life but it was vital to Jimi, and the blandness of the British diet drove him mad. The clubs would usually provide us with some beer and sandwiches backstage, which kept us going, but it was always hard to find a meal after the show because everywhere was shut.

We had started smoking a little dope by then, provided someone else was paying since it was far too expensive for us to buy it for ourselves. We used to worry about the smell getting out from under the hotel bedroom doors, although I doubt if anyone in the hotels we were in would have had the faintest idea what it was. It helped us relax and unwind, but certainly didn't help take the edge off our appetites, in fact it made it worse. I always had to roll Jimi's joints for him because he was so fumble-fingered when it came to that.

Right from the beginning of our relationship I was aware that Jimi was a terrible flirt and that I had to keep my eye on him. One night we were doing a gig at a club in Manchester and I went into the Ladies, not having noticed that Jimi had disappeared. It was a typical cheap club with damp walls and a Ladies consisting of a row of flimsy cubicles and basic handbasins with grubby bars of soap and no towels. While I was fiddling with my make-up at the mirror I heard all this whispering going on in one of the cubicles. I listened for a while and realized it was Jimi with some girl. I could see their legs under the door. I pushed the door of the cubicle open and found them both standing there with their clothes in disarray, looking very shocked and guilty.

'What the hell do you think you're doing?' I screamed at Jimi, terrifying the poor girl out of her wits.

Jimi gurgled and stuttered for a few moments in search of an explanation. 'We were just talking,' he said eventually. 'She wanted my autograph . . .'

I was furious and went on shouting and screaming at him for some time, which he always hated. He was annoyed at finding himself in such an embarrassing situation but couldn't think of any way to get himself out of it. I didn't speak to him at all for at least the next twenty-four hours. He must have decided to be more cautious in the future because I never caught him red-handed again, although I knew he would happily hand out our telephone number to any girl he met.

Towards the end of the tour I gave up going with them and stayed in London, unable to stand the boredom a moment longer, and consequently I gave him his freedom to mess around with anyone he wanted to away from home. Any musician who has toured will tell the same story of how tedious it is to do a show in some poky venue, go back to the hotel in the middle of the night and then set off at the crack of dawn for the next booking, repeating exactly the same exercise day after day. The reason so many musicians resort to drink, drugs and casual sex on tour is simply to try to make the time between shows pass more quickly. It wasn't long before I realized that I was not going to be wanting to go on the road any more, and that I would much rather stay at home in the warm and go out with Angie in the evenings.

Jimi, however, was in his element, despite all the petty irritations and discomforts. I think he was happier during those times, when everything was just starting and he was having to rough it, than he ever was once he hit the big time. He had none of the pressures which arrived with stardom. It was all new and exciting. Most people took no notice of him and there were none of the crowds of sycophants who would later hang around him all the time, flattering him, pandering to his appetites for sex and drugs and driving him mad.

After a few months we had to move house again. Chas always claimed that we had to leave Montagu Square because there was a clause in the lease which said no blacks and that Ringo had been receiving complaints from neighbours. I think it is more likely that the neighbours were complaining about the noise we made when we rolled home in the small hours of the morning. I was always forgetting my keys – I once had to ask John Entwistle to climb along a ledge and get in through one of the windows in order to open the door for me while Jimi was away on tour – so I dare say we woke a few people up from time to time. (I remember John making a great deal of fuss when he was balancing on the ledge, pretending to worry about whether he had enough insurance.)

Chas managed to rent a fourth-floor flat in a modern block in Upper Berkeley Street, close enough for us to be able to move house on foot, carrying our few meagre possessions up the street with us – still mainly clothes, guitars and a record collection. It was a nice flat; Chas obviously had some money coming in by then. Once again, it was taken for granted that he and Lotta would have the best room and Jimi and I would get what was left – managers were often thought of as being the more senior in pop partnerships in those days. We stayed in that flat for about a year or so.

Ronnie Money had taught me how to cook a few things that

Jimi liked, like Scotch mince and tatties, which made domestic life a bit more peaceful. Jimi was often away on gigs or tours and I stuck to my decision not always to tag along, having seen the show time and time again, not to mention the hundreds of hours I had spent listening to them all planning, discussing and jamming. I preferred to go out with my friends or just sit in and watch television with Chas and Lotta who were settling down in preparation for getting married.

Jimi had always said he would love to have a dog. He had had one as a child and still remembered it with fondness. When his twenty-fifth birthday was coming up I decided, without giving it a lot of thought, that I would buy him one. I had heard that basset-hounds were good pets because they slept a lot and didn't need much exercise. My friend Barbara and I went up to a breeder in north London and purchased a sweet-looking puppy with which we duly surprised Jimi.

Jimi was delighted and Ethel Floon became a member of the family. He called her 'Queen of Ears'. Everyone loved Ethel, despite the fact that she was quite incapable of actually hitting any newspaper we laid out for her to relieve herself on and always managed to find a gap with a bit of floor showing. No one had told me quite how stupid bassets were or how impossible to train and she used to tear around the flat with her ears flying out behind her. Sometimes she tripped up on her ears and fell over. I would walk her in Hyde Park for exercise and a number of friends used to help out by taking her down to the country for days out. Back at the flat she had a swivel chair, like the one they used on *Mastermind*, and she loved the sensation of being spun around while she flopped back and relaxed. Once Jimi overdid it so much she staggered off dizzily and threw up on the carpet.

Eventually she grew so big that I realized she was more than we could cope with. A friend, I think it was Trevor Burton of the Move, offered to take her to live with him in the country. We took him up on it, knowing she would be going to a good home. Buying a puppy was a silly thing to do really, and she was too much responsibility for us at that time.

When Jimi went away on tour I was beginning to want some independence as well, and to be able to go out with other people, but I didn't want to tell Jimi about it. I was still only twenty years old and the world was full of interesting and amusing people that I wanted to get to know better. I was no more ready for a monogamous relationship than he was.

Jimi was very jealous and didn't trust me at all – a hangover from the days when his mother left them to go off with other men, I guess – so I had to keep quiet about what I was up to while he was away, which meant keeping it from Chas and Lotta as well since they would have told Jimi straight away if they had thought I was misbehaving. Jimi didn't like me to have anything to do with other men, however innocent the friendship might be.

One night we were having a screaming row on the steps down to the Bag O' Nails Club because he had found me making a phone call and assumed it was to some other man, and John Lennon and Paul McCartney turned up and tried to calm him down. Jimi stamped off in a rage and so I went and sat with Lennon and McCartney.

In fact I had been ringing Angie, but Jimi was always ready to believe the worst. The fact that I would always talk to anyone I knew, whether they were male or female, used to drive him mad. If we were in a club and I saw some people I knew at another table I might join them, but Jimi didn't like that and thought I should stay with him all the time.

That night Paul was talking a lot about Jane Asher, who was his current girlfriend, and the fact that she was off in America somewhere pursuing her acting career. He couldn't understand why she wanted to work when he was perfectly capable of supporting them both. I have to admit that I couldn't see the point of working when you didn't have to, but then I was still very young and I had no idea how much Jane's acting meant to her. Nothing much was happening in the club that night and things were a bit boring so I went home a little later on my own. When Jimi got back there was hell to pay. He couldn't stand the fact that I had even been sitting with someone else and refused to listen to me.

Although he expected me to behave like a saint he wanted to be totally free himself. I was always very good when he was home, curtailing my social activities, quite happy to spend my time with him. But even when I was with him he would flirt with anyone who was around, no matter how plain they were, which I found irritating. If I ever confronted him with an accusation he would simply deny it, his eyes wide with innocence and hurt puzzlement that I should think such things of him.

In fact I wasn't that bothered by the idea of him going with other women as long as it wasn't right under my nose – although it wasn't until after his death that I discovered just how promiscuous he had been. I was very happy with my life and as soon as I saw him and Chas climbing into the car outside the house, heading for the airport, I would be on the phone to Angie or one of my other girlfriends: 'They've all gone,' I would shout gleefully, 'get round here!'

By the summer of 1968 Jimi was topping the bill at the Woburn Music Festival at Woburn Abbey. The craze for big outdoor events was only just starting and organizers still had a lot to learn. After Jimi came off-stage a group of us went back to his caravan for a drink. The security was very poor and the fans managed to break down the feeble temporary fences which were supposed to keep them out. The first we knew was when they hit the side of the caravan like a tidal wave, pounding on

the walls. Then they began to rock it from side to side, screaming, 'Jimi, we love you!'

We were all smoking inside and as the caravan began to sway
violently, an ashtray must have slipped off the table on to the
foam-upholstered bench seat. We were all so alarmed by the
crowd outside baying for Jimi that it was a while before we
noticed that the seat was on fire and the van was filling with
smoke. We had to choose between choking and burning to death
inside or being torn to pieces outside. We opted for escape. The
roadies drove a car up to the door and held the fans back, hustling
us through while they fought the fire behind us.

Security for pop stars was almost non-existent in those days
and we would often come out of gigs with fans throwing themselves at the car, beating on the windows and roof. The drivers
would just have to keep edging forward and hope that they didn't
crush anyone under the wheels. It was terrifying as you saw the
fans' distorted faces being squashed up against the glass by
the force of the people behind. I'm still amazed nobody got
killed.

We all smoked a lot in those days. Nobody was concerned
about the dangers to health. When we had no money we used
to smoke cheap brands but as we got more sophisticated we
moved on to the fancy king-sized brands. Jimi liked smoking
elegant mentholated cigarettes like St Moritz which had white
filters with gold bands round the top – a long way from his
wild-man image. He had a beautiful gold Dunhill lighter someone gave him which he promptly lost, like everything else. I did
smoke but I never became addicted, always able to stop and start
whenever I felt like it.

On one of Jimi's trips to America I gave in and agreed to
meet him in New York. I realized my mistake almost as soon as
I got there. I hated being stuck in hotels, surrounded all day
and night by hangers-on. They all seemed so aggressive and

in-your-face. I felt uncomfortable away from home among a crowd of people I had nothing in common with.

Luckily I ran into some members of Traffic we knew and Dave Mason told me he was flying back to London the next day. I said I would go with them. Jimi was too stoned and out of it by that time to notice what I was doing. We drove out to the airport, only to discover that Dave had forgotten his passport, so we had to get back to Manhattan with all our luggage and instruments in the back of the car. Killing time before the next flight, we went to the Scene Club but while we were inside, the car was broken into and everything was taken, including Jimi's famous military jacket. It was freezing cold and I had nothing to wear, so they all had to club together to buy me a coat. After that episode I couldn't wait to get back to my own home and the company of Angie and the others.

Having a big flat in the West End of London was perfect for my social life, especially when I was there on my own. Whenever Chas and Lotta were away with Jimi for any length of time, I could bring back anyone I liked after we'd finished at the clubs to play music, talk and smoke dope. Sometimes we'd end up in bed. But it all depended on Jimi not finding out. He needed to maintain the image of me waiting patiently at home for his return. Once, when Paul McCartney was at Montagu Square, Jimi phoned up, wanting to know what was going on and I had to lie and say I was just reading. I was worried that Paul would make a noise and give the game away.

Brian Jones had become very friendly with Jimi after I introduced them, and used to come round all the time. He was often one of the first to ring when he knew Jimi was away. Sometimes his requests were bizarre. 'Kathy, you've got to help me,' he whispered urgently down the phone to me late one night.

'What is it, Brian?'

'I've got this girl here and she just won't leave,' he said. 'Come round and help me.'

'What?'

'Just come. I'll pay the cab fare.'

He was living in a flat overlooking the King's Road at the time. When I got there I found him with this girl who did look as if she was settled in for the night. Brian immediately grabbed me and started nuzzling me as if I was his long-lost love returning after years away.

'What are you doing, Brian?' I wanted to know as I pushed him off, laughing.

'Just go along with me, please,' he hissed.

So I let him sit me on his lap and whisper sweet nothings till eventually the poor embarrassed girl got the message and left. As we watched her from the window she stopped to talk to a policeman in the King's Road. Brian's paranoia took control.

'She's telling him about the drugs,' he shrieked, 'she's telling him everything.'

'Then we'd better clean the place out.' We spent the next few minutes ransacking the flat and flushing everything down the loo. But the police never arrived. When daylight came, and I had gone, Brian must have decided it was safe to stock up again and gone out to score. Later on the police swooped and Brian was all over the front pages of the press.

It was the sort of situation we all dreaded. In those days a drug bust was a serious business – people could go to prison for the slightest thing and careers could be ruined. Brian always blamed that poor girl for shopping him but I've seen her often since and I'm sure it was a coincidence. It was more likely that he was followed to wherever he scored the new supplies, or they were intending to raid him anyway.

Georgie Fame was another good friend during that period and was sharing a mews house with Mitch Mitchell. Georgie and I were in bed one night at his place when there was a frantic knocking on the door downstairs. Georgie was panic-stricken when he peeped through the curtains and spotted Nico London-derry, with whom he was having a secret affair. He dashed down-stairs to head her off while I held my breath upstairs for what seemed like for ever before I eventually heard the front door close. Georgie came back looking very pale. In the end they were married amid a squall of newspaper headlines and, much later, Nico tragically killed herself by jumping from the Bristol suspension bridge.

I was always very nervous of Chas finding out about what happened in the flat while he was away, since I knew that he was still looking for a way to persuade Jimi to give me up in favour of someone less independent-minded.

As soon as Jimi came back home my social life would stop for a few weeks because he would have had enough of that on tour and would be wanting a quiet, domestic time with just the two of us. I was happy with that, too, for short bursts, and it was never long before Jimi had recharged his batteries and was ready to start socializing again.

Everyone in music circles had started smoking dope regularly now that they were all becoming more prosperous, but we were constantly paranoid about being busted. Everyone, that is, except Lotta, who never touched anything like that. Jimi was always horribly careless whenever he was carrying anything, leaving it loose in a pocket where any policeman could find it. Sometimes, while he was away, I would put my hand down the side of the sofa and find a big lump of dope he had completely forgotten about, there was so much of it around.

In 1967 acid was just starting to be introduced into London and there was a lot of gibbering from people like Jimi and Brian about how they were expanding their minds and seeing new insights into the meaning of life. They would listen to the most inane psychedelic music and read great things into it. I listened to their fantasies and wondered what on earth they were talking about. Most of the time they just bored me and whenever I tried acid it made me feel ill and out of control.

As he got more into drugs I would sit and listen to Jimi giving interviews, spouting the most ridiculous acid-inspired stuff which the journalists would soak up as if it were timeless wisdom. Like most acidheads he had visions and he wanted to create music to express what he saw. He would try to explain this to people but it didn't make sense because it was not linked to reality in any way. That would frustrate him and he would take more acid in an attempt to get closer to recreating his visions, but the more he took the further away his goal drifted. '1983' had this strange rushing, buzzing noise going through it, just the sort of sound you hear when you are tripping. He also talked a lot about the 'other side' and about death, which people later interpreted as being about suicide but was really only about being in an altered state of mind.

We were sitting on the bed together when he read me the lyrics for '1983'. 'So my love Katherina and me decide to take our last walk through the noise to the sea, not to die but to be reborn, away from lands so battered and torn, for ever . . . What do you think of that?' he asked when he'd finished.

'I'm not coming with you,' I told him, making him laugh, 'you can go to the bottom of the sea by yourself.'

The first time I found Jimi's LSD it was in a little brown eye-dropper bottle in the fridge at Upper Berkeley Street. He was away somewhere and I didn't know what it was. It didn't have any smell so I started to pour it down the sink when Barbara, a girlfriend I had met in the clubs, saw what I was doing and stopped me, suggesting we should try it instead. I didn't much like the result. We put it on blotting paper or a sugar lump and ate it. I only swallowed about a quarter of the amount anyone else would have taken because I hated being out of touch with reality. I like to be in control of what I am doing.

But that was nothing compared to what happened one night at the Speakeasy. Jimi had gone on stage, leaving his Scotch and Coke at our table. Without thinking I sipped at Jimi's drink while he played. I began to imagine I could actually see the music going round the room and it was becoming unbearably loud until I thought my eardrums would explode. I noticed that the faces of the people around me were moving and distorting horribly and I began to become very afraid. I have always had trouble with asthma – Brian Jones and I once had to share an inhaler when we were together – and I began to struggle for breath. By the time I had slipped under the table, Eric Burdon had come back where we were sitting and confessed that he had spiked Jimi's drink with LSD for a laugh. I staggered out on to the steps outside, followed by a concerned Angie, frightened by the way the ceiling seemed to be coming down on top of me.

Someone called an ambulance and I was taken to St George's Hospital, overlooking Hyde Park Corner, where I saw sabre-toothed lions and tigers coming out of the walls. Everywhere I turned there were more of them stalking towards me. The nurses pulled up the bars on the sides of the bed and I cowered behind them all through the night, the walls and ceiling alive with ghouls, unable to breathe and suffering extreme paranoia. The next day the police were by my bed, trying to find out who had 'forced me' to take drugs but they didn't manage to get any further with their investigations. From then on Jimi was fiercely protective and would never let anyone give me anything.

Mostly it just seemed like harmless fun, like the night I came out of the Bag O' Nails with John Lennon and we drove around the streets in his chauffeured Rolls, smoking a joint and giggling. I was more shocked by the fact that he stopped the car at a telephone kiosk and got out to pee in it than by any of the drugs he did. I felt it was a disgusting thing to do somehow and it almost put me off him as a person.

At another party at a girl's flat in South Kensington, a guy called Terry the Pill, who had been the Animals' roadie and had remained very friendly with Eric, fell asleep with his mouth open. Lennon and I, giggling like a couple of naughty schoolchildren, dripped LSD down his throat from a dropper. We waited eagerly for Terry to wake up, floating on the ceiling, but he was made of far sterner stuff than that. When he finally did stir he didn't suffer any apparent ill effects at all. His system must have been so full of drugs our contribution simply made no difference, a mere flea bite on the back of a rogue elephant.

Lennon used to come round to the flat when Jimi was away, usually to get stoned, and just crash out. One evening he spent several hours tripping on the floor behind the sofa and never spoke to anyone, being completely paranoid and frightened because he was in a strange place. You could have a laugh and a drink with John but I always found him too domineering to be really likeable.

Jimi's great hero was Bob Dylan. I think they only met once, in New York, and were both too stoned to do much more than grin at each other. When he brought the *John Wesley Harding* album back from America we played it over and over again. Jimi particularly loved a track which went: 'I dreamed I saw Saint Augustine, alive as you or I' but felt that it was too personal to Dylan for anyone else to be able to cover it. Then he thought he would do *All Along the Watchtower* but he was terrified that Dylan would laugh at him and the critics lay into him.

'Just do it,' I told him, 'don't worry so much.'

He got together a bunch of musicians, including Dave Mason and Brian Jones, who turned up with the most enormous sitar, and we headed down to the studio in Barnes. As soon as he got there and started playing, Jimi realized he had brought the wrong guitar – it wasn't quite the tone he wanted, or something – and sent me back in a taxi to get another one. When he finally got going the music just flowed out of him and even Dylan has been quoted as saying that on the resulting track, Jimi had made the song his own.

Jimi would often book studios himself when he was in London and we would go down with any bunch of musicians he could raise. I used to roll joints and lie on the long padded bench seat behind the console and fall asleep, we were there so long. They would jam together for as long as they could manage. Sometimes Mitch or Noel would be there if Jimi was able to get hold of them but he was happy playing with anyone. I used to get quite bored just sitting there while they messed about for hours.

We used to go to the Olympic Studios in Barnes a lot. I would ring up the engineers there, one of whom was Eddie Kramer, to try to persuade them to let us have as many hours as possible. Most of them were all right, but Eddie never liked us to stay too late because he wanted to get home and he objected when we smoked dope in the studio. He used to complain about our crowding the place out and partying. Jimi would often take over and do the mixing himself. It would cost something like thirty pounds an hour. We would stay for three hours or so and then I would write out a cheque for Jimi to sign.

I didn't have a bank account of my own, but then I didn't need one as most things were done in cash or on account. We had credit at the Speakeasy so we could eat and drink there whenever we wanted and the bill would be sent on to the office. The same happened with the telephones and every other kind of household bill. Jimi had an account which he only used for getting cash out. He once sent me into St Martin's Bank in Edgware Road to draw out £3,000 for something (the equivalent of about £60,000 today). The bank manager wasn't happy about letting a vulnerable girl out on the streets with so much cash on

110

her and sent someone to walk me the few blocks to the flat.

It was bliss not to have to worry about money on a day-to-day basis, to have everything paid for and be able to do more or less whatever I liked most of the time. Occasionally I would run out of cash while Jimi was away, and then I would just ring the office. They would track Jimi down and get him to authorize whatever I needed before giving it to me. If no one could find him I would go to Harold Davidson, who was Jimi's promoter, and his people would advance me the cash.

We got on much better with Chas once we were at Upper Berkeley Street, partly because Jimi and I weren't rowing so much by then, being more used to living together, and partly because there was more money around and everything was easier. Added to which Chas and Jimi were away a lot. We bought a better stereo and Chas used to bang on our bedroom door to tell us to turn the music down, but otherwise things were pretty harmonious for a while.

However, Chas was beginning to suspect that I was not leading as quiet and domestic a life as he would have liked when they were on tour. He had heard rumours and became worried that I would mess up the flat if I wasn't controlled.

'I've lent our room to Tony Garland and Madeline Bell while we're in the States,' he mentioned casually, just before he and Jimi left for a three-month tour of America.

'Oh, fine,' I said, trying to sound just as casual, and to hide my horror at the prospect. Tony Garland was on the management payroll as Jimi's public relations man and Madeline was already established as a singer. I didn't know either of them well and I felt sure they were being planted in the flat to spy on me and make sure I behaved. It looked like my wings were being firmly clipped.

When Tony and Madeline arrived I already had my friend Barbara staying and the atmosphere was a little chilly. I made sure I didn't do anything wrong to start with and gradually, as the days went by, Madeline showed herself to be such a friendly person that we began to grow close. In the end we were having the wildest times ever.

Over the following hectic weeks, Madeline became one of my best friends. She was a great cook and we were able to eat better than ever before and the flat turned into a regular hang-out for a lot of musicians like members of Procol Harum and the Move as well as people from the old crowd like Brian Jones and Keith Moon. A couple of musicians were up at the flat one night before they were due to go to Brest in France to do a gig. They left at about three in the morning to catch their flight and after we had waved them off Barbara and I decided to see if we could get there before them. We dashed down to the airport, managed to get a flight and were waiting for them at the arrivals gates in France. Not only had my wings gone unclipped, I was flying further and higher than ever before.

When it came time for Tony and Madeline to go there were a lot of tears and sad farewells. We didn't know exactly when Chas and Jimi were due back, so they returned to their own place and Tony waited to be told the arrangements.

At six o'clock one morning the phone rang. Barbara and I were fast asleep. Struggling to come to the surface, having gone to bed only an hour or two before, I picked it up. It was Madeline.

'I've just heard,' she said, 'they're on a plane now, they'll be home in about four hours.' Mad asked was the place spick and span. I said no, there were empty bottles, full ashtrays and a bag of rotting chips we'd nicked from outside the Wimpy.

Half an hour later she, Barbara and I were dashing through the flat at a hundred miles an hour hoovering, polishing, dusting, binning the mountain of booze bottles and even cleaning the walls and windows. With just minutes to spare Madeline dashed home, Barbara left and I climbed back into bed so that I could give the impression of having just woken up when they walked in. I heard the door open and voices outside the bedroom.

Chas sounded surprised: 'This place looks better than it did when we left. It's a good job Tony and Madeline were here to look after it.'

What I didn't know was that over the next few months, as he became one of the biggest stars in the world, Jimi would become increasingly difficult to deal with, refusing to see anyone else's point of view or take any advice but his own. At the end of the next American tour Chas flew home before him. I was in the bedroom when he arrived back.

'Kathy,' he said, with a face like thunder, 'pack your stuff. You and Jimi are out.'

7

'My relationship with Jimi is finished,' Chas told me, furious. 'I'm no longer his manager. You'll have to find somewhere else to live.'

'We haven't got anywhere to go,' I protested.

'That's your problem,' he snapped, obviously wanting nothing more to do with us.

Not knowing where to start, I went round to a local estate agent and explained that I had to find a flat to rent in central London.

'Is this for you?' the agent enquired.

'Yes,' I said, 'for me and my boyfriend, Jimi Hendrix.'

'Oh my God.' The man put his head in his hands. 'If you want something anywhere around Mayfair and this area you are going to have trouble. It doesn't matter how much money you've got; the moment it's known who you are, residents' associations will hold meetings and decide that they don't want a pop star living in their building because of the trouble you're likely to bring with you. They just imagine loud music and drugs busts and streams of girls hanging around outside with autograph books. I'll try to find something but it won't be really upmarket.'

I went to look at a few places with him, all of them very expensive, but he was quite right: no one wanted us. Jimi had become a star and everyone had heard of him. His flamboyant image was too powerful – these people would never have believed me even if I had told them what a quiet, gentle man he could be when he was at home. The other problem was that I had no idea how much Jimi could afford or what his management would be willing to pay. I just knew I had to sort something out before he arrived home in England. I went back to Chas and told him I couldn't find anything.

'Well you have to go anyway,' he said. It was plain that whatever had gone on between them had been the final straw. 'And get all Jimi's stuff out of here too. I've booked you into a hotel while you're looking for a flat. The Park Hotel in Earl's Court.'

Earl's Court, which had seemed like the epicentre of the world when I first arrived there from Derby, sounded an awfully long way out now that I had grown used to living in the centre of town, but I could see that Chas was serious and at least it would give me a bed and a roof while I continued my search. I didn't know what to do with all the stuff we had started to accumulate at Upper Berkeley Street, like clothes and records. It was no longer a question of Jimi travelling the world with one sports bag and a guitar. We might not own a lot, but it was more than would comfortably fit into one hotel room. I rang a friend called Carol, who was living with Graeme Edge, and told her my problems.

When Carol told Graeme and fellow Moody Blue, Justin Hayward, about our plight they offered to store our stuff at their flat, which wasn't much more than a couple of glorified bedsits in Bayswater. They sent a couple of roadies to Upper Berkeley Street to pack up all our gear and took it to their rooms.

I went to look at the Park Hotel and was horrified. Chas was adding insult to injury. It made the Hyde Park Towers look like the Savoy. The bathroom was on the second floor. Our room was a great open space with two tiny narrow iron beds, stained net curtains and bare lino on the floor. It had no phone, just a payphone on the ground floor. The moment I got back into the fresh air I rang Carol to describe the full squalor of the place.

'You can't stay there,' she said. 'Come and stay with us while you sort yourself out. You can have our sofa bed.' I was deeply grateful.

Every day we would go through the property pages of the evening papers together to see what we could find and a few days later Carol spotted an ad for a flat to let in Brook Street, just round the corner from Bond Street and Claridge's. She phoned on my behalf and made an appointment for us to go and view.

We met the leaseholder, a guy called Tony Kaye who ran a trendy restaurant on the ground floor of the property called Mr Love. It was a converted Georgian house with two floors of offices above the restaurant and a flat at the top of a little stair-case. It needed painting and was only partly furnished but it had a nice feel about it, cosier than our last two homes, with a modern fitted kitchen and a pink bathroom.

'I have to tell you,' I told Tony, 'this is for Jimi Hendrix, the guitarist.'

'I don't care who it's for,' Tony said cheerfully, 'as long as you pay the rent.'

'Right,' I said, 'we'll take it.' The rent was thirty pounds a week, which was a lot of money in 1968, but it was just what we needed and by this stage I couldn't have cared less about the cost. Chas and Jimi had put me in this position and they would just have to pay and sort it out between them. I had to have somewhere to live and I decided this would be it.

What really tickled us was that George Frideric Handel had lived there – there was a plaque in his honour on the front of the house. It was later that we found out he had actually lived next door. It seemed fitting that Jimi, one of the greatest musicians of his day, should live in the same style. There were other parallels between them. Not only were they both musicians, they had both had to come to England from their own countries in order to find recognition and build international careers.

Now that I had a roof over my head, the only problem was furniture. We didn't even have a bed of our own at that stage, let alone carpets and curtains and all the other things that first-time homeowners suddenly find they have to acquire. I had never put my mind to buying furniture before and I wasn't sure where to begin. It seemed like the sort of thing we should do as a couple, so when Jimi arrived back from America in July I booked us into the Londonderry Hotel in Park Lane for a couple of days and we set off to do a bit of shopping. We got a bed delivered and went to choose all the basics that we needed, which included turquoise velvet curtains and flame-coloured carpets – very unusual colours at the time. Jimi enjoyed choosing the colours and textures and discussing them with the sales staff. Other shoppers stopped and stared in amazement, not expecting to see Jimi Hendrix discussing patterns in the curtain department of John Lewis's. Jimi left me with £1,000 to pay for everything, which seemed like a fortune, while he went back to the States to resume his tour.

'What happened with Chas?' I had wanted to know. 'He was so pissed off with you. Why did he sling us out?'

He would say nothing. It was through third parties that I found out it was the acid, and arguments over his producing and controlling his own music that split them apart.

As far as his career went he was always complaining about something. If it wasn't Chas and the management putting pressure on him to record things he didn't want to record, it was the fans asking to hear stuff he didn't want to play. His ideal situation would have been to be able to get up on-stage in front of huge crowds and just jam away like he used to in the clubs, among friends. The demands of having to do things he didn't want to put enormous pressure on him. Quite often he would swear at the audience if they called out for 'Purple Haze', or 'Hey Joe', or 'Wild Thing', or simply turn his back on them and jam away to the back of the stage.

Later Chas told me how impossible it had become to get Jimi to do anything in America. Chas would tell him that he had to get into the studio to lay down some tracks and Jimi would just shrug and say, 'Yeah, when I feel like it.' Sometimes he would disappear for days on end and then he would invite different people to be his manager or producer or take part on his albums, none of whom his actual management wanted. He would make glowing promises he couldn't keep to anyone who happened to be around. He always had a tendency to tell people what they wanted to hear. If someone he was talking to liked jazz, Jimi would tell them he was planning to do more of it. If they liked blues he would say he was going to move more in that direction.

He also had real difficulty in saying 'no' to anyone about trivial things and when he finally got round to it, perhaps because they started to take advantage, he would do it in an insulting and abusive way, having suddenly reached the end of his tether. He evidently thought he had a better handle on things than Chas, and had managed to push Chas beyond the point of no return.

It was a big mistake on Jimi's part because Chas had always been completely on his side. He had been the first person in a position to do something for Jimi who really believed in his talent. Chas had delivered on all his promises to make Jimi a star and hadn't ripped him off in the process, as had many other managers their protégés. Perhaps the problem was that Chas was too blunt and outspoken. There was no way he would have indulged Jimi with the flattery, hypocrisy and sheer bullshit that later hangers-on came out with. Jimi had started to believe that he didn't have to put up with anyone else's opinions regarding his music except his own.

The pressures of dealing with Jimi took such a toll on Chas's health that he developed alopecia, losing great chunks of his hair. Jimi could do that to people, alienating them completely and then a few months later using his charm to win them back. By the time he was ready to talk to Chas again it was too late: the ties had been broken and Chas was cautious about having anything more to do with him.

Angie, meanwhile, had gone one step further than me, as usual, and had actually married Eric Burdon. In his autobiography Eric says he was turned on by the fact that she was Anglo-Indian: he had made himself a promise at an early age to 'have a deep, meaningful, long-lasting, memorable, erotic affair with at least one member of every ethnic racial group'. He also claims he fell in love with her when she was sitting on some stairs at a party in a low-cut T-shirt and he saw her breasts. Angie's main complaint about the wedding was that they had to drive off afterwards in the group's van with her bundled in the back among all the amps and speakers. Their relationship had been going fine for about two years; their marriage lasted about six months, if that.

The advantage to me of their splitting up was that Angie was available to spend time with me again. I still enjoyed her company more than anyone else I knew. I really loved being with her; we understood one another perfectly. We hung around together again and she still had her wicked sense of humour. When she heard that there was a Turkish baths in the basement of the Dorchester Hotel where a bunch of butch masseuses gave authentic Turkish massages, she insisted that I go there with her and took great delight in pointing out how excited the women got when massaging us, particularly the tops of our legs. They were very professional women, although I objected to the

119

way they pushed us into the cold plunge pools after we had just got out of the hot ones and were studying the ice floating around on the top prior to making any decision about immersion. But I have never again found anyone who was able to give quite such a good massage as those women. It was painful at the time but afterwards you felt absolutely fabulous. For a while we became regular customers.

We used to go to the Indian Tea Centre for breakfast, and for lunch to the Curry Club in the Strand where all the Anglo-Indians gathered to reminisce and eat curries. Angie knew just what to order. I could never understand what anyone was saying at the club but Angie told me, 'You just need to put a "p" in front of every word.'

In those days it was quite hard to get good curries in England and Angie and Mavis taught me how to make them. If we needed a quick meal Angie would boil some eggs and chop them up with curry powder. She called it her 'curry in a hurry'. She turned me into a curry addict long before Indian food became as popular as it is today. She used to like aubergine or prawn pickles spread on bread like a sandwich filling, straight from the jar.

Angie and I decorated the flat together once Jimi had gone back to America. We bought a sofa from a second-hand shop and a table. We got in a decorator and hung all our pictures on the walls. We were like a couple of kids playing house. It was lovely. The floor turned out to have a serious slope to it, making the windows two and a half inches higher on one side than the other, which the soft furnishers hadn't noticed, so they had to take the curtains back and alter them. The wall of the house was bowing out dramatically and has since had to be braced. It gave the place character but made measurements difficult. We pinned Jimi's Victorian shawl to the ceiling above the bed as a canopy and used a colourful Persian wall hanging as a bedspread.

Jimi and I had bought black, red and orange cotton sheets (not satin as some fans believe), which all faded with each successive wash. When he was there Jimi was always good about making the bed and tidying up himself.

I had everything ready for Jimi's return to the country in January 1969. When the day came I hired a limo – a job I was getting practised at – and headed down to Heathrow. Each time the routine was the same: Jimi would emerge from among the other passengers, guitar in one hand and travel bag in the other, his main luggage left for others to deal with. The car would be circling outside, waiting to sweep us up when we emerged into the daylight.

He was absolutely delighted with everything we had done. 'This is my first real home of my own,' he said, and I knew just how he felt. For two and a half months we revelled in having our own little place where Jimi could get off the roller coaster of fame and fortune and hide himself away. We were right in the heart of London, but for a while nobody knew we were there. We were able to be like any other young couple, watching *Coronation Street* together (Jimi was a great fan of Ena Sharples) and drinking milky tea rather than Scotch and Coke. There wasn't even a doorbell at street level so no one could drop in on us without making a prior arrangement. I knew how fragile our tranquillity was; that if ten people came and knocked on the door Jimi would let them all in, regardless of whether they were friends or just passing weirdos. I used to make a point of keeping the downstairs door closed when he was playing music or had his earphones on, ensuring that unwanted visitors couldn't get to us. The noise of the Brook Street traffic made shouting up to us impossible.

Since we had no neighbours, Jimi was able to set up his amplifiers and play to his heart's content. People used to shove notes through the street door saying that they had called but couldn't

121

get a reply. I would slip the notes into my pocket before Jimi saw them. I wanted to keep the world away from us for as long as possible.

Whenever Jimi went away on tour Angie would come round and more often than not end up staying the night. One morning we were woken from a deep sleep by the sounds of someone shouting.

'Miss Etchingham!' The voice sounded quite close. 'Miss Etchingham, are you all right?'

I clambered blearily out of bed to find that some people from the offices downstairs were on the stairs outside our front door. 'What's the matter?' I asked.

'We found your passport down here as we came in,' they said. 'We thought perhaps you'd been murdered or something.'

'My passport?' I could make sense of the whole thing. 'Angie,' I shouted, 'you'd better get up, there's something going on here.'

As the fog of confusion began to clear we realized that we had been burgled. While we were asleep in bed two men must have opened the door with a piece of stiff plastic and had been wandering around the room opening and closing drawers and cupboards, taking my glasses and my passport from the bedside table. They had helped themselves to the stereo and some Persian rugs, even pens that were lying around. It had been going on inches away from us and we hadn't known a thing about it. The thieves had been so laden down with our stuff, they hadn't noticed that they had dropped my passport on the way out. It was frightening.

We reported it to the police and they told us that we were lucky not to have woken up and seen them. We never got any of the stuff back, and I got a lot of new locks for the doors.

My half-sister, Jean, contacted me during this period. She had been widowed unexpectedly and needed help with the funeral expenses. She had found our number through my brother, John, who was living in New Zealand by then. Jimi told me to send her the money straight away. He was always very generous like that. Money meant very little to him. It was there to be spent.

Jean sounded as if she was in a bit of a state, not having expected her husband to die while their children were still young, and so I decided to get in touch with Lil for the first time in six years. It wasn't that I had deliberately ignored her for that long, the lapse had just evolved.

When I first escaped to London I wanted nothing to do with anyone from my past, not even over the telephone, besides which, telephone calls were expensive and I needed my meagre wages for other things. I certainly hadn't wanted to see them. By the time I felt more kindly disposed towards them, having been with Jimi for a while and realized that there were plenty of families that were worse than mine, I was so busy with my own life that I just didn't get round to contacting them. I was always a lazy letter-writer and people didn't use telephones quite as casually then as they do now. At the back of my mind I thought that if I got in touch I might be sucked back in and I just couldn't see the point of it.

Lil was very pleased to hear from me and, as I had feared, said she would like to come down to London to visit me and meet Jimi. A few days later she arrived at Euston station and came to stay at the flat. She was still the same vain, self-centred woman I remembered, but it no longer bothered me in quite the same way. She was so determined not to let anyone find out how old she was that she wouldn't even let them put her mother's age on her gravestone. She used to subtract fifteen years from my age as well. Once, later on, she told a group of people I was about to have my twenty-first birthday when I was thirty-five years old.

'Don't tell people that!' I protested once we were alone.

'Why not?' she wanted to know. 'You don't look a day over eighteen!'

'People aren't that stupid,' I insisted, well aware that I did not look twenty years old any more.

Of course Black Nana was just the same and had died because she told doctors that she was eighty-two when in fact she was ninety-six, and they performed an operation which killed her. Had they known her true age they would never have given her an anaesthetic.

Lil and Jimi got on brilliantly which was a relief. Two gypsies together. He didn't want to go out anywhere while she was there and was very gracious, dashing about opening doors for her and buying her barley wine, which he had never heard of but which she told him was her favourite drink. Lil was a very outgoing person who could chat away to anyone, and Jimi was always good at communicating with people's mothers (he took to Noel Redding's mum in much the same way), making them feel that he would like to be their adopted son. Both Jimi and I were hungry to sample relationships like the ones we felt we had missed out on with our own mothers. I was very pleased to let him and Lil get on with it.

We took her out to dinner at a restaurant in Maddox Street called the Mad Ox. It was a bit of a strain; I felt I had to entertain her, I couldn't just light up a joint whenever I felt like it. I found I didn't hold a grudge against her for the sort of childhood I had had; I just saw it as my bad luck to have her as a mother. Once we had re-established contact we kept in touch sporadically, which meant I would ring her about once a year.

'Oh, Kathleen,' she would say, 'I'm so glad you've rung, I've been really ill . . .' and then she would launch into a monologue about herself and her ailments. All that was required of me was to grunt, 'Oh yes? Oh dear! That's terrible! Poor you!' and other relevant phrases at the right moments. She never stopped to ask how I was or what I had been doing.

She would never talk about the past and what had happened to us as children. If I tried to raise the subject she would wave her hands about and squeal as if I was trying to put a rope around her neck. 'Ooooh, Kathleen, don't talk about it! Don't talk about it! I could never live with your father,' she would wail, 'he was a horrible man.' But Dad could never have been a horrible man, he wasn't capable of being anything, he just didn't have the energy.

Gradually people got to know where we were living, mainly because Jimi would hand out the address to anyone who asked. It became impossible to dam the steady stream of visitors who trekked up the stairs whenever the main entrance was left open and rang the doorbell every time there was a break in Jimi's music. Many of them would want to sell him stuff, like ridiculously overpriced jewellery which he would buy just to make them happy. One of these salesmen, Tommy Weber, used to visit a lot with his tall girlfriend, Charlotte Rampling, who I rather liked. She was already a film star, having been in *Georgy Girl* with Lynn Redgrave.

On one occasion a girl called Caroline Coon arranged to come and interview Jimi for some magazine. When she arrived at the flat she had two people with her, one of them a photographer. After I had let them in she asked if there was somewhere where she could get changed.

'Yeah,' I said doubtfully, 'use the bathroom upstairs.'

She took a bag of clothes up to the bathroom and must have laid them out before coming down to talk to Jimi. They chatted for a bit, making good-natured fun of the fact that her name was 'Coon', and then she said, 'I'd like to have some photographs taken with you, do you mind if I get changed?'

'Changed into what?' Jimi asked.

'Oh, I've got this black underwear that I want to wear,' she said. Jimi immediately lost his temper and told her to get out of the flat. She insulted him back and he went through the roof, shouting abuse at her. Their voices were so loud I could hear them through the floorboards even though I had disappeared upstairs. I wasn't surprised. If Jimi ever felt he was being insulted or asked to pose as if he were some kind of clown, his wrath was terrible indeed.

'You think you're such a big star,' she yelled, 'you think you're above the rest of us!'

I ran downstairs to see what all the commotion was about and saw Jimi hustling all three of them towards the door, screaming furiously at them, 'I'm not having my picture taken with you, you ugly bitch! Get her things from the bathroom!' he told me.

I ran back upstairs and scooped up all the underwear which she had laid out along the edge of the bath. Once the incident was over I never thought any more about it until nearly thirty years later when I saw a diary piece in the *Evening Standard* which said that Caroline Coon had been thrown out of Jimi Hendrix's flat because he was offended by her name. Furious that history, even a trivial incident like this, could be so distorted, I rang the journalist and told them what had really happened. Tony Brown, one of Jimi's biographers, then rang me to say that he had found some magazine pictures from 1969 of Caroline Coon wearing skimpy black underwear, posing with Noel and Mitch. The caption under the picture said that Jimi had refused to be photographed with her. I was very grateful to Tony for providing proof which would set the record straight and demon-strate that I hadn't imagined the whole scene. Many other people would try to change events surrounding Jimi once he was dead and couldn't answer back. Caroline Coon had also claimed that Jimi had answered the door to her stark naked and that the table had been covered in drugs. I remember that I answered the door that day, and I know for sure that I would have tidied away any dope before letting a visitor in.

The next problem was the telephone, which never stopped ringing. I had two phones installed, one with a number which we gave out to people and one which we kept private, and then I would take the general phone off the hook. But Jimi started giving the other number to people in case they couldn't get through on the first line, which completely defeated the object.

Musicians used to come to Brook Street, as they had to Upper Berkeley Street, to visit, and one frequent and welcome caller was Roger Mayer. Roger was an experimenter for the Royal Navy Scientific Service, working in the field of vibration and acoustic analysis systems. I never completely understood what he did, I just knew that it was extremely technical and that he was a nice guy. He and Jimi were on the same wavelength, so to speak, talking about the sorts of sounds, feedback and distortion that Jimi wanted to achieve and adapting all sorts of electronic equipment to make the guitar sound different. I had to stand for hours with my foot on the pedal while they fiddled about with knobs and switches. Every now and then they would tell me to press the pedal, but I could never work out what they were talking about.

It irritated me in later years when I heard that people like Eddie Kramer – the recording engineer at Olympic Studios – had been credited with 'creating' Jimi's sound. I had always thought that Roger and Jimi had invented it, using what were at the time state-of-the-art electronic techniques for underwater warfare. Unlike Eddie Kramer, Roger was a close and personal friend. He used to go down to the Speakeasy and other watering holes with Jimi, discussing all the possibilities of electronic sounds.

Apart from moaning now and again that he wanted to move in new directions with his music, but that his management and record companies wouldn't let him, for those few months Jimi seemed very contented with his life.

One day there was a ring at the doorbell and I answered it to find a fluffy microphone on a stick being pushed into my face and bright lights shining in my eyes. For a horrible moment I thought it was a police raid.

'What do you want?' I demanded defensively.

'We're a film crew,' they explained, 'from Los Angeles. The door downstairs was open, so we came up.'

'Does Jimi know you're coming?' I asked.

'Yeah, yeah,' they assured me.

'OK,' I said, 'I'll ask him.' I went ahead upstairs, assuming they would wait by the door, but they followed me into the room.

'There are these guys here,' I started to say but the lights were already in the room and the microphone was waving around between us.

Despite the fact that Jimi appeared to know nothing about them and just laughed as they pushed their way in, they spent the next few weeks following us around and filming. It's obvious from the way we are dressed that we weren't expecting them that day, but they did capture the feeling of our relationship at the time, very relaxed and happy together. I've heard that they are still trying to release the film but can't get Jimi's estate executors to agree. I can't understand why because apparently the fans are keen to see it. There is also another film called *A Roomful of Mirrors*. It has Jimi speaking from the heart about his childhood and his personal problems. Again, the estate will not agree to its release unless they can edit it. I was pleased that Jimi was now confident enough to tell the media that I existed, but was unsure about having these people intruding into my life.

The two men making the film were both called Gerry – Gerry

Jimi at the Speakeasy; he
could put as much into a jam
session as at a paid concert
(courtesy of Chris Morphet)

'Do you really want an encore?' Jimi at the Saville with Mitch and Noel *(courtesy of Chris Morphet)*

(courtesy of Chris Morphet)

'Damn, where's the fuzz box?' *(courtesy of Chris Morphet)*

At the launch party for
Grapefruit, with Brian Jones,
we looked as though we'd
been fished out of the Thames
(Tony Brown Collection)

'Don't like the look of the canapés.'
Me and Jimi at a reception for Mary Hopkin
at the GPO tower *(Tony Brown Collection)*

How I looked at the time I met Jimi

'Not another one who wants to feel my gonk!' Keith Moon with fans
(courtesy of Chris Morphet)

The Who at the Saville Theatre *(courtesy of Chris Morphet)*

The Samarkand, 22 Lansdowne Crescent, the basement where Jimi died
(*Tony Brown collection*)

Dolores Cullen with Mitch Mitchell at Jimi's inauguration into the
Rock 'n' Roll Hall of Fame (1992) (*courtesy of Candace Carrel*)

Gold and Gerry Goldstein. Gerry Gold had his wife with him and her blonde head seemed to get into every shot.

One day they wanted to film Jimi opening the boot of a car and being surprised at finding the cameraman inside. They asked me to get him to do it without letting him know why. I tried but it was impossible.

'Jimi,' I said, playing along as best I could, 'help me get some things out of the boot of a car downstairs, will you?'

'What car?' he wanted to know.

'Just a car.' Jimi smelt a rat.

'What things do you want out of it? Who's car is it? What are you doing with "things" in someone's car?' He wasn't fooled at all.

Nothing I could say would persuade him to go downstairs, so after about twenty minutes someone had to let the cameraman out because he was having a fit of claustrophobia.

They also filmed two Albert Hall gigs which Jimi wasn't too happy about because it meant having the lights up in the auditorium, which he thought spoilt the atmosphere.

The continuity of the film is very muddled. I fractured my ankle coming home late one night, stepping awkwardly off the front doorstep as Jimi fiddled with the key. As a result I am in a plaster cast and on crutches in some shots and not in others, and our clothes keep changing from shot to shot. It is all very amateurish by today's standards, but it is evidently still a valuable document because of its rarity value.

After the concerts I always used to collect up all the flowers which Jimi had been given and take them home to put in vases. I couldn't bear to see them left around on the floor or in the dressing rooms. After one of the Albert Hall concerts we climbed into the Rolls which was to take us back to the flat so that we could freshen up before going on to a club, and I was laden down with bouquets. When we got to Park Lane we discovered that the entrance to Upper Brook Street was cordoned off. The driver went round to Oxford Street in the hope of getting down South Molton Street, but that was sealed too. We drove on to New Bond Street and found yet more cordons but, as this was the closest entrance to the flat, we decided to get out and walk.

It was a freezing cold night. I was wearing a skimpy outfit with a bare midriff and Jimi was still in his flimsy stage clothes. As we walked to the barrier a policeman came forward to block our way.

'What's going on here?' we asked.

'Never mind what's going on,' he said, shooing us off, 'just move along.'

'Wait a minute,' we protested, 'we live here.'

'Oh really?' he asked, looking suspiciously at the mountain of flowers I was peering through, probably thinking that we did not look like typical Mayfair residents. 'And what might your name be?'

'My name is Jimi Hendrix,' Jimi said, looking embarrassed.

'Anyone here heard of a Jimi Hendrix,' the policeman shouted to his colleagues, 'says he lives round here?'

'I know who Jimi Hendrix is.' Another policeman came forward and peered at Jimi. 'He does look a bit like him,' he admitted. 'What have you got in that case?' He pointed at Jimi's guitar case, possibly imagining that it was some sort of machine-gun. Jimi showed him his guitar and a more senior officer was found. They then gave us an interrogation on our address and telephone number and details of the flat while we stood shivering in the night air. Eventually they agreed to let us through and we were escorted all the way to the flat by six policemen. When we were ready to leave again we had to ring someone to come and accompany us back out through the cordons. The reason for all the security was that President Nixon was staying at Claridge's, just down the road. We had to go through the same rigmarole when we returned in the early hours of the morning and there was a new shift of policemen on duty.

By this time a lot of people, like the policeman, recognized Jimi from his appearances on television and from interviews. When journalists came round I would usually hide myself away but sometimes I hung around to see what was going on, trying not to be noticed.

Jimi quite enjoyed being interviewed and filmed, although he tended to waffle on a lot and put his hand in front of his mouth and giggle rather girlishly. It was hard for him to think of anything deep and meaningful to say to blokes in suits with microphones, but he was always willing to do his best.

He didn't go in for a lot of preening before photo sessions, but he would worry if he had spots on his face. In the end his hair started to give him trouble too. He had had it straightened so many times to get the effect he wanted that the ends started to break off. He began letting it stay more natural, giving up on the rollers, just putting a bandana around his head and wearing a hat instead. It still looked pretty wild.

Sometimes the journalists would ask him questions about politics and race relations because Vietnam and the civil rights movement were in the news. We hardly ever thought about these things. They seemed so remote and didn't really affect our day-to-day lives. Jimi didn't seem to have any clear-cut political ideas, just a vague belief that everyone should try to get along with each other.

Some of the black activists, on both sides of the Atlantic, used to criticize him for having a white girlfriend, which made him very angry. One night, in his early days in London, Michael X, whom we met in a club somewhere, a black activist who modelled himself on Malcolm X, invited Jimi round to his place in Notting Hill, a room with walls covered in Zulu shields, animal skins and African sculptures. Michael himself was a light-skinned West

Indian. We went together and Michael X started berating Jimi for being in a mixed relationship, telling him he should stick to his own people, saying, 'We need people like you to show the way!' We kept looking at each other as if to say, 'Let's get the hell out of here – this guy is obviously bonkers.' And racist. We nearly fell down the stairs in our haste to escape.

I later found out that Michael X was going out with a white woman who was in publishing, so either he was a complete hypocrite or he liked to use white women for some sort of revenge on their race. He was eventually executed in Jamaica, after being found guilty of murdering his girlfriend and burying her body in the back garden.

On the whole we had very few problems with the racial issue. The worst that would happen was that taxis would sometimes drive past and pretend not to have seen us. If more than a couple did that, Jimi would disappear into a shop doorway and I would hail a cab on my own. When it stopped I would open the door and half get in, so that they couldn't take off, while Jimi followed quickly behind.

Within the music business it didn't seem at all strange that we had different skin colours. There were plenty of couples like us, Madeline Bell and Tony Garland being one of them. 'It's got nothing to do with the colour of your skin,' Jimi would say, 'it's what's inside that counts.'

When Don Short of the *Daily Mirror* asked Jimi about me in an interview, Jimi said, 'Kathy is my past girlfriend, my present girlfriend and probably my future girlfriend. My mother, my sister and all that bit. My Yoko Ono from Chester.' I thought he was being soppy.

I actually agreed to do one interview on my own, for *Queen* magazine (now *Harpers* & *Queen*) because they wanted to produce a photo feature on girls whose partners were rock stars. I was reluctant when they first approached me but then I heard that one of the women was going to be Yoko Ono, so I thought if she was willing to talk it would probably be all right. A photographer, I think he was called John Marmaris, came with all the modelling lights and umbrellas and took some very nice pictures. By that time we had some money and I used to buy my clothes from Browns which had just opened across the road in South Molton Street. Brook Street was very convenient for shopping as it was right in the centre of the most fashionable shopping area of town.

Our eating habits had changed too because we were no longer dependent on my primitive attempts at cuisine and could go out to eat at the Speakeasy. We hardly ever went to the fashionable new restaurants that were opening. Jimi was happiest with Madeline Bell's cooking because she would make things like smothered pork chops, fried chicken and corn bread with potato salad. Typical black American food. One night, when Madeline had come round to cook and hang out, Jimi appeared from the bathroom upstairs looking wide-eyed and, as Madeline put it, 'as pale as Jimi could manage'!

'An old guy in a nightshirt and a grey pigtail just walked through the wall while I was standing there!' he said. I thought he was joking to start with but then I realized that he was really shaken. I don't know how much he had smoked that evening but he remained convinced that he had seen Handel's ghost.

Living without Chas and Lotta, Jimi and I could relax and be ourselves more, and Jimi was able to settle down and read his science fiction books and the daft magazines, like *Mad*, he had brought back from America. He loved British humour and was a complete Goons fan, a show most Americans would have found completely incomprehensible. He was seeing more of Mike Jeffery now, too.

Once Chas had handed responsibility for Jimi's career over to Mike, the two of them started to get on again because there was nothing for them to fall out about. Mike Jeffery was the proverbial absent manager, but when he was in town we used to go to his flat in Jermyn Street and sit around drinking and laughing.

Some of Jimi's biographers have painted Mike as the monster who ruined Jimi's life but that wasn't quite the case, or at least didn't seem to be at the time. He may have taken all the money and hidden it offshore somewhere, but that didn't worry Jimi as long as he had enough for his immediate needs. He was only interested in his music and having the freedom to play what he wanted, when he wanted. In the beginning, Mike and Jimi got on pretty well whenever they were together. I think by staying out of the way Mike avoided becoming too familiar with him. Always being in one another's pockets had created too much of a strain on Chas and Jimi's relationship. Later, when the drugs began to get a hold and Jimi's paranoia increased, he began to view Mike in the same way as he had Chas. Mike started trying to make him be disciplined and produce commercial work, just as Chas had done, and Jimi gradually grew to hate his interference. Jimi was impossible for anyone to manage.

It is certain that Mike was syphoning off the money and depositing it somewhere abroad because when I complained to his assistant, Trixie Sullivan, that the rent hadn't been paid she turned up at the flat with a briefcase stuffed with American dollars. She peeled a few off and gave them to me before snapping the case shut and disappearing again.

When March arrived and Jimi was due to go back to America, he asked me to go with him and I agreed, conveniently forgetting just how much I had hated it the last time. But I could have had no idea just how much worse it would be this time around.

8

I went to America partly because Jimi wanted me to and partly because Angie was over there with her new boyfriend, but I wished I had followed my instincts and stayed at home. He told me that every time he left his hotel in New York it was 'like stepping on to a roller coaster'. I had been warned, but in fact it was worse than that: the roller coaster came right into our room.

I flew out a few days after him. We were booked into the Garden Suite of the Pierre Hotel, a fancy place on East 61st Street at the corner of Central Park, and when I arrived there was a huge limousine with darkened windows waiting for me at the airport. It was from a company called Head Limousines. The driver was sucking on a joint and passing it over his shoulder to me as he drove down into Manhattan. In the Big Apple the rock and roll dream had become a constant reality. If you chose to, you could avoid real life altogether.

Jimi wasn't at the hotel when I got there so I settled down after the long flight in the hideously decorated room, in front of the first colour television I had ever seen. The wallpaper was printed with green trellis-work complete with vines growing up it, the sort of pattern which, during the seventies, took root and flourished in every cheap hotel in the world. Outside the sealed picture window in the sitting room was a tiny water garden consisting of a few rocks with a green spotlit fountain dribbling steadily in the middle. I peered up to see if I could see the sky above this little garden, but there was none: it was as fake as an exhibit in a public aquarium.

I was just dozing off when Jimi arrived back, trailing an enormous entourage like the colourful leader of some circus freak show. From that moment on there never seemed to be less than twenty people hanging out around us. If we stayed in the room, they stayed with us; if we went out to eat, they all came too – at Jimi's expense.

They were the loudest, nastiest bunch I had ever come across. Many of the women were obviously whores and the men all appeared to be pimps and drug dealers, with their cool shades and little spoons hanging round their necks like badges of office. I was startled by how relaxed Jimi seemed among them all, a king presiding over a court of fools. If I tried asking him to send them all away, he would become defensive.

'These people are my friends,' he would say.

It was clear that they disliked me, Jimi's 'tight-assed white English bitch', just as vehemently as I disliked them. Many of them were incredibly anti-British, claiming that as Jimi was American that was where he should be, and saw me as a threat, someone who was trying to lure their property away.

One of the gigs that the group was due to do was a concert in Central Park. When the time came to leave we were ushered to two limousines which were to take us through the crowds. Mitch, Noel, Jimi and I were in one and the security people followed in the other.

'The crowds have broken through the barriers,' our security people told us. 'It's going to be hard to get into the venue without being trampled.'

Their plan, therefore, was for Jimi and the security men to rush in first, with Mitch and Noel bringing me in second. The

136

cars stopped, the doors opened and we struggled out into the noise and jostling. Jimi and the security guys disappeared into a sea of people and the three of us put our heads down and ran behind. I was hanging on to Mitch and Noel's arms for dear life, genuinely frightened by the numbers of people pressing in on us. As we neared the gates the police charged forward and one of them hit me in the stomach with his baton, winding me and making me let go of Mitch and Noel who were then whisked inside, leaving me behind in the crowd as the gates slammed shut in my face. Fighting to stay upright, frightened I would be crushed to death if I stumbled, I fought my way out of the park and hailed a cab back to the hotel.

Back in the safety and nightmare decor of the Garden Suite, with Jimi and the rest all gone, I caught my breath and thought about my situation. It was time to make a serious change. This was no longer the sort of life I wanted to lead. The Pierre Hotel was a long way from the fleapit hotels and working-men's clubs of the north of England where Jimi and I had started out, but it didn't seem that much better. I might be able to order anything I wanted from room service, but I certainly wasn't enjoying myself any more, and I didn't have any control over my day-to-day life. It was as boring in its way as hanging around backstage in Newcastle or Manchester – only the food had improved.

The next day a man called Krantz turned up at the room with a sports bag. In my memory he looked like the TV detective Columbo. He even had a limp because, he proudly told everyone, he had been shot in the leg. He was as obnoxious and unattractive as all the rest. He casually dropped the bag on the floor as he lounged among the loud-mouthed groupies and hustlers who welcomed him into their midst, and it gaped open. Inside I saw a large handgun lying on top of hundreds of packets of white powder and my mind was made up for me. I wanted to get as far away from that room and those people as possible.

137

I rang the airline and tried to get a flight out but I was told that I would have to wait at least a few days. Transatlantic flights were not as numerous in those pre-Concorde times as they are today. My first concern was to get out of the Pierre, even if I couldn't get out of Manhattan, so I packed up my case and headed over to Angie's hotel. But things weren't much better there. Her boyfriend, the heir to some fortune or other who liked to live in hotel suites, was heavily into cocaine and had persuaded Angie to start snorting coke and smack.

It was like a nightmare. Everywhere I went the people I loved were doing stupid things, under the influence of vile strangers. I couldn't understand why they couldn't see through their suppliers and yes-men. Why couldn't they see that drugs were changing their personalities and, depending on the chemicals involved, making them nonsensical, boring, paranoid or aggressive?

Once my friends started getting seriously involved with drugs they immediately became dependent on others. Their whole lives revolved around where the next lot of stuff was coming from. I wanted to get out and party, but they couldn't go anywhere until they'd got their stash. They spent days waiting for unreliable flakes and criminals to turn up. Snorting coke also meant that they couldn't get to sleep at night because they were so high and had to take sleeping tablets by the handful.

I did try coke in New York to see what the fuss was about and it just gave me the uncomfortable sensation of being speedy and made my nose run. I even had a snort of pure heroin to counteract the effect of the coke and that made me physically sick for days. I couldn't understand why anyone would want to put themselves through it. Later I discovered that everyone feels like that to begin with and you had to persevere – but why? It seemed insane. I couldn't see the point of these white powders and the alarming things they did to your system.

Luckily Angie and her man had plenty of room in their hotel suite so at least I had some peace and quiet for a while, away from all the madness, as I tried to organize an escape flight back to England. Angie's man did not grow on me at all during the following few days. He didn't seem any different to the liggers hanging around Jimi, just richer. He was showering Angie with expensive gifts and she was loving it.

But I wasn't safe in the suite for long. On the second day I was there Angie came rushing out of the bedroom. 'Quick, Kathy, we've set fire to the mattress. We've had to dump it, there's going to be security all over the place!'

I looked out to find that they had hurled the smoking mattress out of their bedroom window into Fifth Avenue, where it was no doubt causing a considerable and smelly obstruction. It wasn't long before the police were banging on the door and the management threw us out. We had to move to another hotel. The nightmare was growing worse and I prayed, harder than I had since leaving the nuns, for a seat to come vacant on a plane out of there, any plane.

Eventually my prayers were answered. I think I had to fly Irish International via Shannon and change planes twice, but I had got away from New York and that was all that mattered. The flight was packed with priests and nuns going to Ireland and when it hit violent turbulence they all crossed themselves and prayed in unison. I was so relieved I almost joined them.

I really missed Angie when I got back to London, much more than I missed Jimi, and I was certain that New York was not good for her as long as she was surrounded by drugs. I felt that if we could get her away the old Angie, the one who was fun to be with, would resurface. Her family were worried about her too, so I cooked up a plan with them to get her back to London before she got too far into the drug scene and became as

139

permanently messed up as the other cokeheads and idiots I had met in New York.

Her sister, Betty, rang Angie and told her that Mavis, her mother, had suffered a heart attack. Angie took the first plane she could get a few days later, miraculously finding her mother much better once she returned. She was so aggressive and hyper at the time that we didn't pluck up the courage to tell her the truth for many years.

Getting her out of New York seemed to have broken the spell, at least for the time being. She decided not to go back and to dump the dreadful heir. Angie and I knew each other so well that we were more comfortable together than we ever were with our boyfriends. We both still resented it when the other got into a relationship with someone else if it meant that we couldn't spend as much time together as we wanted. That was why my relationship with Jimi was so perfect for us, because it left us with time for ourselves. We had so much fun together.

Angie was attracted to men who offered a little danger. A year or so later she took up with Arthur Lee, a well-known black musician, on a visit to Los Angeles. After a while she came scurrying back to England complaining that Arthur was always playing with guns, spinning the chambers while snorting coke. When he held a gun to her head even Angie could see it was time to leave. In 1995 Arthur was given a long prison sentence for various firearm offences, after brandishing a weapon during an argument with a neighbour and firing a gun in a public place.

Even before the Arthur Lee incident it was a relief to be back in England and away from people with guns. The group, Traffic, had a cottage in the country where they used to go to rehearse and Dave Mason or one of the others invited us down regularly. We had wonderful times there, driving around the Downs in a Land Rover at a forty-five-degree angle as if we were about to roll over, like a ride at the funfair, or lying around in a house so far away from the rest of the world that the group could rehearse at full volume on the patio without annoying the neighbours. We were free and happy. It was what everyone believed the sixties should be, before the hard drugs and the money and the paranoia really kicked in.

We didn't go to clubs as much any more because most of the people we knew were earning a lot of money and could afford to buy big houses in the suburbs or the country and throw lavish parties. Even Keith Moon ended up entertaining his friends in a desirable residence, complete with a swimming pool, but he was still as wild and loopy as ever. One night at his house, where he was living with a girl called Kim, several of us were sitting around in the sunken lounge when we heard a commotion out on the patio. Running outside we found that Keith had driven his Rolls-Royce into the pool. The car was nose-down in the water and Keith, dripping wet, was sitting laughing on the side. Somehow it didn't seem that funny to me. I wondered if I was growing too old for that sort of thing.

Keith was so crazy by that time that even those of us who loved him used to try to stay out of his way. It was a case of 'Oh God, here comes Mooney', whenever he was spotted approaching. It was sad because we were all so fond of him, but you don't always feel like being bear-hugged, lifted off the ground and whirled around in the air. He once came up behind me unexpectedly in the Speakeasy, putting his arms around me with such force that I vomited violently. I later found out that he could have ruptured my spleen. Even though I was all right I was very cross with him, scolding him like the out-of-control puppy he was. He simply didn't know his own strength and had more energy than he knew what to do with.

In the past Jimi had never been one for going around with the lads. He had always much preferred the company of women. He liked hanging out with me and Angie, and with Madeline when she and I became close. He particularly liked 'Miss Madeline', as he called her, because of her cooking.

I don't think he ever really realized how close Angie and I were. He didn't understand that we could criticize each other and get away with it in a way other people couldn't. He was always very defensive of me if he heard her or any of my friends running me down. Angie and Carol were having a whinge to him about me one day and apparently he listened carefully to everything they had to say, then stood up and banged their heads together, telling them never to talk about me like that again.

Getting out of a taxi in Brook Street in July 1969, I saw Chris Farlowe sitting at a table on the pavement outside the Mr Love restaurant.

'Hello, Chris.' I went over to him, fishing around in my bag for my front-door key.

'Have you heard the news?' he asked.

'What news?' I asked, not really listening.

'Brian drowned in his swimming pool last night.'

I was so shocked I didn't know what I felt. By the time I got up to the flat the phones were ringing and everyone was swapping stories and rumours. None of us could believe what had happened. This was the first time that someone close to me had died and it didn't seem real. Was it drugs? Was it murder? Was it suicide? A hundred different theories were circulating and there was probably an element of truth in all of them. Brian Jones was one of the characters who had started the whole rock circus rolling, but there was no real place for him in ordinary life.

After Angie and I got back from New York Jimi went very quiet, ringing only infrequently. I imagined he was so wrapped up with the huge tour he was doing that I had drifted out of his life. It seemed as if we had both moved on. I knew that he was seeing other women – I had a clear mental picture of the sort of ghastly females who had been lounging around the Garden Suite at the Pierre – so I assumed he had become involved with someone else and that he and I weren't really a couple any more. It didn't bother me unduly; it seemed like a natural progression of the relationship, the same sort of progression I had made with Keith and Brian. My affair with Jimi was certainly the most important I had had so far, far deeper than any of the others, but there was no reason to be surprised that it was drawing to an end. After all, I was still only twenty-two years old.

One night, down at the Speakeasy, Angie met a guy called Ray and told me how nice he was, very laid-back and handsome with a great body. I felt the familiar pang of jealousy at my best friend going off with some man and leaving me to fend for myself, but that was nothing new. Then I started to get to know Ray and he and Angie stopped seeing each other after a fairly short time. He and I gradually became an item and it was Angie's turn to feel left out. I started to like Ray a lot and after a few months of going around together I found that I was completely besotted with him.

Ray's father had a successful interior-decorating firm, with contracts at places like Buckingham Palace because of their expertise with gold leaf on plasterwork, and Ray worked with him. The family seemed comfortably off. The only blemish in Ray's character was that he drank too much. At the beginning of the relationship that didn't matter; it just added to the fun. I preferred that to being with cokeheads.

We spent Christmas with his family and I felt very warm and comfortable about the relationship. It was so much steadier than anything I had ever had before. I no longer felt any desire to be part of Jimi's 'roller coaster' life. I felt I was growing up, but I couldn't quite find the courage to tell Jimi how I felt or that I had met someone else. I suppose I thought that if I just said nothing his calls home would become less and less frequent until eventually they disappeared altogether, or he would tell me that he had met someone else and I would be let off the hook.

I felt slightly guilty, chatting away on the phone to him about what I had been up to and hearing his news and how tired he was, but leaving out the most important thing that was happening to me. At the beginning of our relationship the thing I had liked most was that we could tell each other everything that was happening to us, everything we were feeling. It was sad to think that that was no longer the case. Now it seemed to me that my first priority was to sort my own life out, and I was quite sure I couldn't rely on Jimi in the long-term: there was just too much going on to be able to predict what his future might be. If I sat at home waiting for him to come back I might still be sitting there in twenty years' time. I had to rely on myself, just as I had always done. I was sure he could look after himself. He had always given me that impression, anyway.

At the beginning of 1970, encouraged by Madeline, Ray and I decided to get married, buy a house and settle down. Ray more or less moved into Brook Street with me while we were house-hunting. The flat was in my name because I had been the one who was around to sign the papers, so I could give it up whenever I felt ready.

I didn't want a big, fussy wedding; I certainly couldn't imagine myself in a virginal white dress, so we planned a low-key, pleasant day among friends. Madeline and Tony were there, probably Angie, Lil and a few of Ray's family. Lil thought Ray was great – 'so handsome', just the sort of man she approved of. I wore an angora trouser suit with a matching hat and scarf.

I hadn't heard from Jimi for a while and apparently he was having problems. He had a disastrous gig at Madison Square Gardens and walked off-stage. Around this time someone must have told him about me getting married to Ray. He rang to find out if it was true.

'Yes, I'm married,' I told him, innocently. 'Is there anything you would like to keep from the flat because I'll be giving it up. We're buying a house in Chiswick.'

'I don't know what I want,' he said, his voice sounding strange, 'I'll have to think about it. Are you going to be there next weekend?'

'Yes,' I said, assuming he intended to phone back then. Ten minutes later he called to tell me he would be flying into London on the Saturday and asked me to pick him up at the airport. I agreed, surprised, and booked a limo to Heathrow as usual. Jimi turned up on the early-morning flight looking a complete wreck. I was amazed to see that he was alone because I had never known him to travel without some sort of company before. On the way back into town he held my hand in the back of the car.

'This is just a spur of the moment thing, isn't it,' he said, his voice quiet and intense. 'It's not serious, is it?'

'Yes, it's serious, Jimi,' I said, 'I'm married to Ray and I love him.' I was startled to see how completely devastated he was by the news. I suddenly realized that he had pictured our relationship completely differently. He may have been sleeping around in America but he hadn't met anyone else he wanted as a permanent partner. He had imagined that I would be waiting for him, the good little woman keeping the home fires burning until my man came back from earning our living – not so very different to Chas's idea of how relationships should work, after all. He hadn't realized that we had drifted apart. He still saw us as a couple and he simply couldn't believe that I had moved on. I realized that in his mind I had let him down just like his mum and dad had before me. He had been relying on me to be a permanent fixture in his life, but I was nowhere near old or mature enough to fulfil that role. I wasn't willing to give up my life to be a rock and roll widow.

Ray had gone to work by the time we got back to the flat and I made tea.

'So,' I said breezily, 'is there anything you want from the flat?'

'I don't want to take anything from the flat,' he said angrily, with tears in his eyes, 'I want you.'

'Does anyone in New York know you're here?' I asked, trying to keep the conversation light.

'I don't have to tell them everything,' he replied, his head hanging down, his whole body looking limp. 'Why don't you come back to New York with me?' he suggested.

'I can't do that, Jimi,' I said.

'Why not? We can go back, everything will be all right, all those people I was hanging out with have gone.'

'No, Jimi,' I interrupted, 'it's not going to happen. Everything is different now.'

He kept arguing for a while but I knew he wasn't going to change my mind. I could never have gone back to the life I'd had with him. I wanted to move on to something different, away from all the mayhem and madness. A lot of our friends were starting to pair off and disappear from the club scene, we were growing up, but that would have been impossible for me if I had stayed with Jimi.

I told him that Ray had moved into the flat with me so he couldn't stay there and I booked him into the Londonderry Hotel. After the first couple of days of trying to persuade me to change my mind he seemed to realize that I wasn't going to budge and gave up. He jammed in the studio with Stephen Stills and Graeme Nash one day and that seemed to lift his spirits. On another day he asked me to go shopping with him and bought me a pair of snakeskin boots. We were like two very old friends on a day out together and I felt a wave of relief that he had come to terms with what had happened. It was over but we could still be part of one another's lives. At the end of the week he went back to America.

He had showed no interest in the stuff left at Brook Street except for a few things which he took back to New York. So when the time came for me to move I had to decide what to keep and what to throw away. There was a cupboard which was stuffed with all the paintings and drawings Jimi had done during his time in London, many of them inspired by acid. I had no idea what to do with any of it, so I binned the lot, except for a drawing we had done together. Many of the old wall hangings we had bought had started to disintegrate so they went out as well. It didn't occur to me that one day they would be of any value or interest.

In July 1970 Ray and I moved into a nice little terraced house in Chiswick. I learnt to drive and got myself a job which I really enjoyed. I was happy in my new role of young wife and normal citizen when, a month or so later, I had a call from Angie.

'I'm at the Londonderry Hotel,' she said, her voice sounding panicky, 'with Jimi.'

'Jimi's in London?' I was surprised, no longer having any idea of his movements, as we hadn't spoken to each other for six months.

'He's here to do the Isle of Wight Festival. He's gone mad, Kathy, we need your help. He's thrown us out of the bedroom and he won't let us back in, and all our clothes are in there. He's shouting at us to get out but we're trapped in the suite. We were all getting on fine and then he just turned on us. You're the only person we can think of who can deal with him when he's like this.'

I took a taxi to Park Lane and went up to the suite. Angie and another girl, wrapped in blankets, were waiting in the wrecked sitting room. Broken lamps, smashed glasses and upturned tables bore witness to the rage that Jimi must have

147

been in. I went through to the bedroom. The first thing that hit me was the heat. It was a blazing hot day outside but all the windows were shut and a blow heater was going full blast, making the air feel dry and uncomfortable. Jimi was lying in bed under a pile of blankets, shivering uncontrollably. There was an empty bottle of Jack Daniel's and some glasses on the bedside table.

'What's happening, Jimi?' I asked.

'What's happening, Kathy?' He sounded as casual as if I had just come back from popping out to the shops.

'Angie and that girl need their clothes, man,' I said. 'They're scared to come in here.'

'Give them the clothes, get rid of them.'

I scooped up their clothes and took them out to the sitting room. The girls dressed hurriedly. Watching them, I felt so glad to be a married woman. I felt detached. Once they had gone I went back into the bedroom to see if I could do anything to help Jimi. I sat on the edge of the bed and put a cool flannel on his forehead to try to bring his temperature down. He seemed to be dangerously feverish and kept sniffing and complaining that he had a cold. He was thin and grey and looked really ill. I assumed he had a bad dose of flu. In retrospect it is obvious that he was suffering some kind of withdrawal symptoms, although I'm not quite sure what from.

I made him as comfortable as I could and, once he was sleeping, I went back home, feeling a great sense of relief that I was no longer a part of this scene, pleased to help but even more pleased to walk away. The distressed superstar in the hotel suite was not the Jimi I had met and fallen in love with four years before. All the sweetness and gentleness had disappeared: the drugs and the stress had changed him beyond recognition.

A couple of weeks later I was browsing around the hippy stalls in the dark, aromatic bowels of Kensington Market, when Jimi came up from behind and squeezed me. He looked fine.

'I'm staying at the Cumberland Hotel,' he told me. 'Why don't you drop by later to say hi?'

'OK,' I replied, 'I might do that.' But I knew I wouldn't. For years after his death I felt guilty thinking that if I had gone to the Cumberland Hotel that night everything might have turned out differently. But I know now that he wouldn't have been there anyway.

9

The next morning Madeline rang me at home and a friend took the call. 'Ask if I can call her back later,' I said, busy with something else. He came back a few moments later.

'She insists on talking to you now.'

I went to the phone, grumbling.

'Are you sitting down?' Madeline asked.

'No,' I replied, laughing, 'why?'

'Get a chair.'

'What? Tell me.' I began to feel worried by her tone.

'Just get a chair and tell me when you are sitting.'

'OK,' I said, a few seconds later, 'I'm sitting down.'

'I just heard on the radio, Jimi died last night.'

I hung up without saying a word. I rushed out to buy an *Evening Standard*, scouring it for news but there was nothing in it. I felt a huge surge of relief – Madeline must have got it wrong. 'Is this the last edition?' I asked the vendor.

'No,' he shook his head, 'one more to come at three o'clock.'

The next bundle of papers to hit the pavement had the story all over the front pages. Jimi was dead, apparently from an overdose, choking on his vomit. The media were gleeful: it was just the sort of death they would have wished on a man like Jimi, who flouted all the rules of social behaviour. It was like the final chapter of a cautionary tale for children.

I read and reread the story, trying to work out what had happened, but none of it seemed to make sense. A huge part of my life had just disappeared without any warning. I began to think what would have happened if I had followed through on his invitation to go to the hotel the night before. Would he have taken the same cocktail of drugs if I had been there? Would I have known what to do when he threw up? The facts in the paper were too sketchy to be able to make out exactly what had happened. I couldn't believe he had gone. I had imagined we would always be friends.

An old journalist friend of Ray's rang up and suggested I write a story of my life with Jimi and sell it to a Sunday tabloid. In my innocence and confusion I allowed the two of them to talk me into it. Why not? It would be a tribute to him, telling people the truth behind the image. I agreed and talked to the journalist at length. He seemed to understand what I was saying. He sounded sympathetic to the story I wanted to tell.

By the time it came out the article read like a nightmare, bearing no resemblance to anything I had actually said. The headlines screamed about drug orgies and sex sessions; it took the wild-man image and blew it up into a monster, a demon rock star as only the tabloid media can create. They had failed to get Mick Jagger and Keith Richards so they went after Jimi who, just like Brian before him, was no longer in a position to do anything about it.

I came across as stupid, hysterical, oversexed and drug-soaked, just another groupie cashing in on my contacts. None of it sounded remotely like anything I had actually said.

It was my first experience of being a victim of the media's insatiable thirst for sensation and it left me profoundly shocked, horrified to think that my friends would believe I had said such things. I suppose I should have been wiser, having been with Brian when the press were persecuting him, but I had never taken much notice of any of it since it didn't affect me directly.

I went to a lawyer, thinking that there must be some way in which an innocent person could protect themselves against this sort of attack. The lawyer was kind and sympathetic but told me I couldn't afford to take on a mighty news organization, and that there was virtually nothing in the story which I could actually sue over. My best course of action, he suggested, would be to lodge an official complaint and then never to give any more interviews to anyone from the media.

I took his advice and remained silent for twenty-two years, except for one US radio show in 1981. This apparently worked well, with me telling stories from our early days about how we had to count the pennies just to buy ourselves a packet of cigarettes, often having to beg and borrow from friends even for that kind of modest purchase. The interview has become a collectors' item and has since been released on a boxed cassette, which was rather a surprise as nobody mentioned that would happen when they first approached me. It was just one more reminder that I could easily lose control of my own past if I let the media past the door.

If journalists managed to find my address and wrote to me asking for information about Jimi, the rock scene or London in the sixties I would ignore their letters. It wasn't a hard decision because none of it interested me any more. It was past and I had moved on to new things; I didn't want to keep raking over the ashes of my early twenties.

Over the next two years Ray's drinking became more and more of a problem. When he was sober he was charming but always wanted to have control over my life, which I wasn't comfortable with having enjoyed so much freedom since leaving home. With a few drinks inside him he would become violent and confrontational if I put up any sort of argument about anything. He was as jealous and possessive as Jimi had been, but with the difference that he was always there, watching my every move, unlike Jimi who had been away most of the time. I felt trapped and just couldn't sort out what I should do about it. I began to hate him for what he was doing to me.

When I bumped into a friend called Dawn, who I hadn't seen for a number of years, and she asked me how things were going, I let it all pour out, telling her that I was married but that it wasn't going well, that I wanted to get away but didn't have anywhere to go, that I had made a mistake but didn't know how to rectify it.

'I've been renting a flat in West Kensington,' she said, 'and I've just bought a house, so if you would like me to assign the lease of the flat to you, you can have it.'

'How much is it?'

'Six pounds ten shillings a week, but it's a big flat, about half a house, with its own garden and everything.'

The flat was as good as Dawn said and it was exactly right for what I had in mind. Suddenly I could see a way forward, an escape route from my situation. I paid up £700 key money and took it over. As with Jimi, I didn't have the courage actually to tell Ray I wanted to leave him, so I pretended that the flat was for both of us, while making sure that it was in my name. I felt bad about being deceitful but if there was one thing my child-hood had taught me, it was to ensure that I had a roof over my head and not to rely on anyone else to provide it. I persuaded him to sell the house in Chiswick and we moved to Lisgar Terrace together; not exactly what I had in mind but a move in the right direction.

By now he seemed to be drunk all the time and I dreaded him coming home. One night he was arrested and the police kept him in the cells till morning. This moved us into a different league and gave me a legitimate reason to begin to break up the marriage which not even his parents could really argue with. I told him I couldn't take any more and that he must leave the flat and straighten himself out if he wanted our relationship to continue. I told his parents that if he didn't give up the drink the marriage wouldn't survive. After a battle he went back to live with them. They hoped they would be able to do something about his drinking, and that once he was sober I would take him back, but I never had any such intention.

We stayed friendly, as I always did with my ex-lovers, but I immediately had all the locks on the flat changed, telling Ray it was because I had lost my keys. I just kept pussyfooting around without ever working up the courage for an all-out confrontation, until he finally got the message.

We saw each other regularly as friends and he no longer seemed to be working for his father. I was aware that he was into some sort of business which was proving very profitable, but I had no idea what it was, apart from the little he told me. To be honest I wasn't particularly interested in his life any more. I didn't need to hear any intimate details which, as it turned out, was just as well.

'We import and export musical equipment,' was all he said, so I left it at that. I noticed that he always had flashy cars and plenty of spending money, and travelled all over the world on business which gave me nice long breaks between our meetings. I was glad to see him doing well and he gave me plenty of money to live on so there was no reason to complain.

Then while he and his partner, Jim Morris, were away in America on business, I received a phone call from Jim's girl-friend, Gay.

'Ray's in trouble,' she said.

'What sort of trouble?'

'He needs to talk to you himself. I'll give you a number but you must call it from a public phone box, not from your own phone.' She gave me an overseas number.

'Where is this number?' I asked.

'Hawaii,' she said. 'Ray will explain.'

It gradually emerged that Ray was on the run from the law because he had been smuggling dope for Howard Marks, a man who was to become notorious as the greatest drug smuggler in Britain. Ray and Jim had been packing huge quantities of dope into speakers which were going round the world on tour with various bands and a colossal load had been found at Las Vegas airport.

Ray told me that he was in a hotel room with Howard and some others in California at the time of the bust. In his book, *Mr Nice*, Howard describes how a reporter came on the television and said, 'Hey, one of you guys out there has just lost five million dollars. Today, law enforcement officers seized Nevada's biggest-ever haul of illegal drugs . . .'

Apparently, one of the speakers had been left behind at John F. Kennedy airport in New York during a transit-plane change and a sniffer dog found it in a warehouse. The customs authorities then intercepted the rest of the speakers in Las Vegas, emptied them of the drugs but let one of Howard's people pick them up, so that they could follow him and see where he went. Another of Howard's contacts was watching, however, and saw the tail, tipped off the driver by overtaking him and dropping a screwed-up brown paper bag out of his window as an agreed signal. The man with the speakers, a hardened Vietnam veteran, then drove round in circles until customs realized what was happening and picked him up. The rest of the team had scattered to different parts of the world, all furnished by Howard with false passports and enough cash to survive for the immediate future. Howard flew back to London, via New York, and Ray headed for Hawaii.

'Now I'm stuck,' he told me. 'I daren't use the passport Howard's given me or they will pick me up. Will you come over here?'

He sounded in bad need of a friend and some moral support so I agreed to go. Gay suggested that I fly to Los Angeles and then get an internal flight from there, so that Hawaii wouldn't appear on my passport when Customs and Excise came knocking on my door.

I had only met Howard Marks once at that stage. For some reason he had turned up at my twenty-eighth birthday party which we threw at one of those riverside restaurants opposite Dolphin Square which were so fashionable at the time, probably the Elephant on the River. I had been struck by how clever and well educated he seemed. Even though I didn't know him he had happily paid for all the champagne which we were merrily pouring down our throats that night. He had a strong Welsh accent which made it difficult to understand what he was saying to start with. By the end of the party we were all doing the conga round the dance floor of this upmarket venue, dragging along a load of people we didn't even know.

I sat next to him again at a dinner party recently, after he had served his time in prison and was planning to write his autobiography. I told him that I envied him his distinguished university education (he achieved a second-class honours degree in physics from Balliol College, Oxford, despite having spent most of his time there experimenting with mind-altering drugs) and the opportunities it had given him, but he waved the idea aside.

'It's all nonsense,' he said. 'I just happened to be good at one particular subject, that's all.'

I told him I was considering writing my life story as well but wasn't sure that it was a good idea.

'Just do it,' he advised, 'it will give you a chance to think about everything again.'

Hawaii sounds, of course, like the perfect place to be hiding out and my first impression of Ray's situation fulfilled the image of being marooned in paradise, complete with huge, deserted white beaches, swaying palm trees, constant sunshine and a laid-back local population.

Ray had rented a condominium just up from the beach on the north shore of Oahu. At the beginning of the seventies this side of the island was still relatively undeveloped. There was one big Japanese hotel being constructed, where we occasionally used to go for cocktails, but otherwise it was mainly populated by surfers, attracted by the giant wave known as 'the pipeline'.

Ray had completed the fantasy by buying an MG sports car, but the joys of motoring around the island in an open-top car were rather marred by the petrol shortage, which meant that we were constantly having to queue up in garages for fuel. The other drawback for me was that I am allergic to mosquito bites, and they were everywhere, even biting my ankles when I was driving. Within a day I was covered in blotches and bumps.

We fell in with a glamorous group of people who all seemed to finance their beach-bum lifestyles by making occasional drug runs in and out of the country. When they weren't transporting narcotics they would just live on the waves or lounge around on the sand, turning themselves as brown as they possibly could. God knows what their skins must look like now, but then they were the colour of perfectly polished mahogany.

I had learnt many years before that my skin did not react well to the sun, so they used to settle me under an umbrella while they all stretched out to fry and bleach their hair so blonde it was almost white. I would turn heads because my skin was bone-white compared to everyone else's.

Our evenings were spent at beach parties, eating and drinking round giant bonfires beside the ocean. I stayed out there for several weeks but soon became bored. Most of the girls in the group had never even been off the island and had absolutely nothing to talk about, while the men sat around wearing bandanas and carrying fearsome-looking guns, semi-automatic rifles which they would occasionally discharge into the air just to watch the trail the bullets made.

Ray agonized constantly about what he should do next. His main problem was that once the money Howard had given him had run out, he would have no way of earning a living in America without a work permit or proper ID. He could see no future for himself in the US.

After endless hours of discussion, swinging back and forth between unmade decisions, we concluded that I should fly back to England and talk to a lawyer on his behalf. The lawyer I found was in no doubt that Ray should return to Britain and give himself up. Ray and I kept in touch from the phone box in Lisgar Terrace.

A few days later, when I was away for the weekend, I got a call from my friend Debbie, who was living in my flat at the time. 'You've been raided by the police,' she told me. 'They've been through everything and taken away lots of photographs and other personal stuff. I told them I didn't know where you were but they want you to go down to the Customs and Excise offices in Fetter Lane.'

I went to Fetter Lane as requested. They wanted to know what I knew, but I had been very careful to ask Ray as few questions as possible about the logistics of his operations and the people involved, realizing that the less I knew the better. The Customs and Excise people obviously didn't believe me and kept me in an interrogation room for hours. There were two of them, one being nice and one being nasty just like in all the movies. They had guessed that I had seen Ray, or at least knew where he was, but I continually maintained that I knew nothing. They showed me pictures of other people they thought were involved in the business, but I didn't recognize any of them. They had my passport and asked what I had been doing in Los

Angeles. I told them I was just visiting friends. Eventually they let me go home, warning me that if I talked to Ray I should persuade him to come back.

When I next contacted Ray and told him what had happened he agreed to return to Britain.

We were all waiting for Ray's flight at the crack of dawn in a deserted terminal. The passengers eventually came through but Ray wasn't among them. A few hurried phone calls revealed that the flight had been full and he had been bumped off it and given $200 compensation. When the message came through via the lawyer that he would be on the next plane, the Customs and Excise officers became exasperated, not believing a word of it, but they did their own checks on the flight and eventually found out that it was true. As Ray came through from the next flight I was horrified to see that they were getting out the handcuffs.

'You don't need them,' I protested. 'He's come all the way from America to give himself up, he's hardly likely to do a runner now.'

Thankfully, they agreed and the cuffs disappeared back into someone's pocket. They let us walk out of the terminal with our arms round one another and have a few words before they arrested him and subjected him to a body search.

When he finally got to court and admitted everything, he was convicted of conspiracy and sent down for four years. The judge seemed more concerned with the fact that he hadn't paid tax on his earnings than that he had been moving more dope around the world than anyone had ever dreamed possible. At one stage the prosecution wheeled in such a massive block of the stuff on a trolley as evidence, it raised a few laughs in the courtroom.

He was sent to a jail in Norfolk and I went to visit him a couple of times. Once I caught a bus from Victoria coach station which was laid on free for prisoners' wives and families. It was a long gruelling journey with the kids all shrieking, shouting and vomiting while their mothers screamed abuse at them. I decided not to do that again. The next time I went up with Dawn in her car and we got lost.

It must be awful for a prisoner to be waiting for someone who turns up hours late, but Ray made such a terrible fuss that I didn't fancy going again.

He kept writing me letters, telling me what to do, and I became increasingly fed up. Ray began to complain that he wasn't hearing from me often enough. He became angrier and angrier until eventually he wrote saying he was going to divorce me, and sent the papers along with the letter for me to sign. I did as he requested and sent them back. The divorce went through without a hitch but when he came out after two years, having been given time off for good behaviour, Ray seemed to think that it didn't count, and that we were still married.

He wrote to the landlord's agents and applied to take over the lease of the flat on the basis that he had paid the rent at the beginning. They wrote back and said that as far as they were concerned his ex-wife was the tenant. I never really spoke to Ray after that. It was a relief.

10

I met Nick Page when he came round to Lisgar Terrace with some letters for my flatmate. Her cousin was a flatmate of his and the letters had been sent to his address by mistake. He was a junior hospital doctor doing anaesthetics and intensive care. He settled down and looked around the flat at the carpets, wall hangings, silk scarves and jewellery. He told me he had been brought up in the Middle East and that when he was a student in the sixties he had driven back out there during vacations, buying up embroidered clothes and accessories which he sold to shops in the Portobello Road and King's Road, probably to the same boutiques that I used to go shopping in with Brian and Jimi. He thought that some of my scarves were his and had come from Aleppo in Syria. He told hair-raising stories of avoiding Syrian army roadblocks in the 1967 war, and of hanging out with Turkish smugglers in Hatay. He came round a couple of times that week and we chatted away.

One day he asked me out for a drink and then I realized why he had been visiting so often. He took me to a bar in the Fulham Road and I was surprised to find that he knew the barman, a man called Josh who was one of the few people to have been attacked by Johnny Bindon and escaped unscathed. Bindon was reputed to be a friend of Princess Margaret and was well known in the area for his violence and tendency to pick fights with anyone he came across. If ever I went into a pub and saw him there I would go straight out through the revolving doors. He seemed psychopathic to me. Angela had known him and he had attacked one of her boyfriends with a broken bottle, getting him right in the balls, necessitating a visit to hospital for stitches. Bindon recently died of Aids.

On the way home Nick put his hand on my knee in the taxi and gave me a clue about what direction he wanted things to go in.

I grew to like Nick more and more. I liked the fact that he was intelligent and I could talk to him about virtually any subject. I had never met anyone so highly educated and highly qualified apart from Howard Marks. He had been to public school and studied medicine at Cambridge but, despite our totally different backgrounds, I felt I was much better suited to his personality than I had been to Jimi's or Ray's. He is entirely unflappable and in control of his own life, while being self-confident enough not to need to try to control me. We used to have rows, just as I had had with Jimi, but they didn't have the same intensity as we discovered that we agreed on most things. I found myself going round to the hospital when he was on call and staying in the cramped room provided for the on-call doctor. I got dirty looks from some of the nurses.

Before long he moved into Lisgar Terrace and we became a couple. One evening two exotic-looking Arab girls from the Lebanon turned up and chatted away in a mixture of Arabic, French and English. They seemed to be old friends of Nick's. One of them told us that her brother had been shot by some Palestinians. As Nick sat cross-legged on the floor and talked to the two girls about Beirut and the street fighting going on there, I realized that he had been closer to much more alarming situations than I had ever imagined.

Nick was getting fed up with being in operating theatres all day and decided to take a sabbatical to think over what he wanted to do next. He had always been interested in marine biology and some friends of his owned one of the largest private islands off the coast of Britain called Scalpay, close to the Isle of Skye. We decided to go up there and help them set up a scallop farm with some Japanese marine biologists.

The island was 10,000 acres of beautiful, wind-blown land with its own supply of fresh spring water. There were several cottages dotted around and we all lived together in a big oak-panelled hunting lodge. Since there were no cars, we would walk or ride horses everywhere and take a sea truck, which is like a military landing craft, to the mainland. We had to grow our own vegetables and once or twice, when the weather was bad, we ran out. The Japanese were very resourceful and willing to eat anything from kippers and nettles to razor fish and sea urchins. Yoshiko, a Japanese girl who went on to become a successful dealer on the Tokyo stock exchange, showed us that very young bracken was not poisonous; 'Mountain vegetable', she called it, but the rest of us thought it was disgusting.

We used to bake our own bread in the Aga and spend our evenings sitting around the kitchen table, socializing with the visitors who would come and go. I did quite a lot of cooking, taking my turns with everyone else except Nick, who was, unbelievably, an even more terrible cook than I. However he would eat anything, like the Japanese. I just followed Mrs Beeton's cookbook – the house had all the necessary equipment. It was a welcome change of gear from London, a chance for us to get to know each other and to take time to think about our lives and where we wanted to go next.

We couldn't get any television and were quite isolated from the rest of the world. In the evenings we used to play games such as Diplomacy, a strategic form of Risk, sometimes not finishing until after dawn. It hardly got dark at all in the summer.

Nick and the other men on the island had a completely

different approach to guns to the men I had met in Hawaii. They used to talk all night about which of the stags should be shot because they were too old or unwell, and would all try to avoid being the one to do it. They used powerful rifles with telescopic sights and would creep silently up gullies and crawl through freezing wet mud for hours to get into the right down-wind position to kill the deer with a single shot. They hated wasting ammunition.

Nick used to go scuba-diving every day, checking on the long lines that held baskets of scallops in the sea. Usually he went with the Japanese or with Ted who lived on a neighbouring island. But once we had to go out alone together in a little rowing boat with a motor. He taught me the rope signals and disappeared over the side, leaving me all alone in the freezing Atlantic Ocean, not even knowing how to start the engine. If I had, I might well have gone off to get help since he didn't reappear for over three-quarters of an hour. I was left bobbing about with a rope in my hand, not knowing what was happening but well aware that I was stranded in an area where killer whales frequently crashed past and storms could blow up at any moment. When he did finally come up he didn't seem to understand why I was so furious with him.

Once the two of us took the boat to go for dinner with a couple who lived on the nearest island to ours. We left them later than we intended and it was dark by the time we were halfway home, with no moon to tell us where we were or to guide us into the harbour. We got home, steering by the stars, and our host, who was waiting on the jetty for us waving a light, was fuming. Everyone had realized that we had disappeared but had no way of knowing where we were. If we had been just a few degrees out we could have been heading for the North Pole, or ended up on the rocks. Luckily it was a flat calm night and Nick could work out our direction from the stars.

After being there a year, we realized that Nick would have to get back to the rat race and we returned to Lisgar Terrace and Nick got a job at the Royal Marsden Hospital.

In 1977 we decided to get married and start a family. This was an even more low-key event than my first wedding – just the two of us and a couple of friends as witnesses at Fulham registry office. We had James seven months later. Nick was the first man I had met who I felt I wanted to have children with. I felt totally safe with him, knowing he would never let me down. I was more in love than I had ever been before.

I know that Nick's parents were rather disappointed when they discovered that he was marrying me rather than a 'lady'. They seemed very grand to me when I first met them, Nick having given me no warning at all about what they were like. They lived in a huge country house outside Chester, filled with beautiful Middle Eastern treasures and surrounded by gardens with views over the forest. I felt totally overwhelmed when we rolled up there and were shown to our separate rooms. I was even nervous about going down to breakfast on my own in the mornings, since Nick's mother seemed to run a very formal household and I was not sure what the rules were. Nick couldn't understand why I was so uptight. I must have seemed pretty common to them at first but one day, when we had been together a few years, Nick's mother was walking with me in the gardens, and she admitted, 'We were quite worried about you when Nick first brought you home, but we have changed our minds and we think you have been a very steadying influence on him.'

His father invited us to a reception of knights in one of the City guildhalls and surprised me by bringing the Queen over and introducing me. I shook her hand and bobbed, and for once I couldn't think of anything to say. All I can remember thinking was that she was much shorter than I had imagined.

At the time Nick and I met, Angie was living with a guy called

Terry de Havilland, a society shoemaker who was very generous and looked after her well. They had a son called Caesar in 1973 but a year later Angie left Terry, got herself a flat in Fulham and met a man who was heavily into heroin. Angie didn't need much encouragement to get back to her old drug-taking ways. Neighbours alerted the NSPCC that Caesar seemed to be a neglected child, and the authorities helped Angie get him into a local nursery school.

Angie gave the school my telephone number as the person to ring if she couldn't be reached, and I would often get a call from them to say that all the children had gone home but Caesar was still there and no one knew where Angie was. At that time I had a new baby of my own to look after, so one of the teachers would generally take Caesar home with her and I would try to find Angie. It wasn't long before the authorities were threatening to take him into care.

The rest of Angie's family had emigrated to Perth in Australia and kept in regular contact with me. They asked me to stop giving Angie money because they believed she was spending it on heroin. It was a hard thing to do as I had always been very open with Angie about everything. Now the only way to avoid the problem was to lie and tell her that we hadn't got any money ourselves.

She never used to tell me directly about the drugs; I would always find out via someone else, or see the evidence for myself. It was almost as if I was her second mother, the one who would be nagging her to kick the habit all the time. She knew that I didn't approve. 'Oh Angie,' I was always saying when the smack withdrawals were making her aggressive and spoiling her life and Caesar's, 'when are you going to get off that stuff, for God's sake?'

'Oh Kath,' she would sigh, 'I'm really going to do it this time, I'm really going to kick it' – all the usual things junkies say.

When James was about four months old I took him round to Angie's flat. The door was open so I lifted the pushchair up the steps and let myself in. I called out to her but there was no answer. I went through to the scruffy kitchen and found her and her boyfriend standing at the table, leaning against one another, both totally oblivious to the world around them. There was a rubber band round Angie's biceps and a needle and syringe still hanging from her forearm. There were splashes of blood on the walls. It was the first time I had seen her in quite such a squalid and hopeless situation.

I turned round and took James straight out. I felt so sad to think that the beautiful, lively girl I had met on her seventeenth birthday had ended up in such a mess. She had always been willing to take risks and push the boundaries, trying things that we all knew were stupid and dangerous and allowing people who were obviously no good to lead her on to new experiences, and now it looked as if she had gone too far.

There must have been something strange in her make-up which made her act like she did because there was certainly nothing in her family background that I could see to cause her to go off the rails. Her family are the nicest, straightest people. If anyone should have ended up in the gutter it was my brother John and me, but it never even seemed a possibility to either of us. Angie had been the greatest friend I ever had, but now I had Nick and James and I could no longer be involved in someone else's downward spiral. I felt that I had moved on, and knew that I was going to have to leave her behind. I still loved her and would probably never have a friend like her again. I realized that we had grown apart as old friends sometimes do, but it made me feel very low.

Although we stayed in touch, standing semi-conscious at her kitchen table was the last time I was to see Angie alive. We had both reached a crossroads in our lives and had chosen to go in opposite directions. Her family persuaded her to go to Australia to live close to them, away from the people she was hanging out with in London. It was a hard battle to get her a visa and she had a great many doubts about whether she would be able to make it, but in the end she managed to get there. She used to write to me from time to time about what she was doing. She told me she had met a singer with INXS called Michael Hutchence who had odd sexual habits, but what really surprised her was when he asked her what it felt like to be 'coloured'. Angie was taken aback by this. She had never thought of herself as 'coloured'.

To start with it sounded as if everything was going to be all right. Caesar went to live with his aunt Betty and they managed to get Angie off heroin. Then she met someone and got married again, although I'm pretty sure that her Mexican divorce from Eric can never have been legal. That sort of detail wouldn't have bothered Angie. But before long she grew bored with her nice new husband and met another guy called Steve, who had also gone out there from England. She fell in love with him and they had two children together. Over recent years, I have been able to piece together what happened. Apparently she started to drink heavily as well as take drugs again. During the very hot weather she didn't have a fridge because she had sold it to finance her habit, so her mother bought her a new one. When Mavis went round the following week Angela had already sold it for a fraction of its value.

'All the welfare workers have told us not to give her any money,' Mavis told me, her eyes full of tears, completely confused and puzzled by what could have gone so wrong with her beautiful younger daughter, 'but I was worried she wasn't eating.'

Every now and then Angie would be arrested for possession and while she was in jail she would straighten out and write to me, starting each letter with: 'My dear friend, look where I am again,' and then going on to make promises that she would beat the addictions this time. 'Steve and I are going to do it together,' she told me in her last letter.

Steve, I later heard, met someone else and threatened to take the children away from Angie. In December 1992 the two of them got into an argument in their kitchen, Angie pulled out a kitchen knife to attack him, he grabbed a knife to defend himself and they started to fight. His knife went into Angie's chest and, according to her mother, 'sliced six inches off her aorta'. She died instantly. Steve pleaded that it was a crime of passion and was sentenced to four years. The children went to his parents because Angie's mum was well into her seventies by then and not able to take on the responsibility.

'Kathy,' Angie often used to say to me, 'you were always more sensible than the rest of us,' and, amazingly, I guess it was true. I had seen how they all behaved in New York, and I knew I didn't want to be like that. I didn't want to be like Brian, Jimi, Keith, Angie or any of the others who tried to escape from themselves and their lives through drugs. I was always more conservative. When they were wearing layers of floating chiffon or antique beaded dresses and flowers in their hair I was in fairly plain Biba dresses and court shoes. It was just my personality. The drugs simply never interested me that much.

All through the years that Angie's tragedy was unfolding on the other side of the globe, I was getting on with my life with Nick. We moved to Ealing and had our second son, William. Nick tired of surgery and became a general practitioner. I was now a respectable doctor's wife and the mother of two fine boys.

I found that having children made me think more about my father. I wondered what had become of him after we lost touch and began to want to see him again, to make contact before it was too late, if it wasn't too late already.

Just before my twenty-first birthday my grandmother had got

in contact with him and told him he ought to give me a gift of some sort. Apparently he had just sold the last of his inherited land and had a small amount of cash. He told Black Nana that he intended to give me a present but that he wanted to give it to me personally, after all the years we had been apart. I was very excited at the prospect and wrote saying I would be delighted to see him. He sent me a letter saying that he would be on the eight o'clock train into King's Cross.

Angie and I went up to the station to meet him. The train came and went but Dad was not on it. He wasn't on the next one, either. As we hung around the station, waiting in vain, I felt desolate. It was my twenty-first birthday and neither of my parents could be bothered to come and see me. All the feelings of abandonment which I had gone through as a child flooded back. I so much wanted him to step off one of those trains, but he didn't.

Despite all the emotional barriers I had erected since I was ten years old, I was crushed to be so let down. I had been sure that this time he would be there for me, but he wasn't. I saw no point in trying to find out why not. What difference would it make? Angie and I had gone back home to her flat in St James's and downed a bottle of whisky between us. I didn't have to explain how I felt to her, she knew me well enough. The next morning I had managed to file the hurt away in its proper place and return to business as usual. I hadn't heard from him at all after that.

Nearly two decades later I decided that I would like to try to see him one more time. I had no idea where he was or even if he was still alive. The last time anyone else in the family had heard of him he had been living in Ireland with the tinkers, but anything could have happened since then. I contacted the Salvation Army, giving them his name, which they took to the DHSS. I also wrote to my aunt Kathleen and both she and the

Salvation Army found an address for me at the same time. He was living with a couple called the Murphys on a council estate outside Dublin, so I wrote to him care of them.

I received a reply from Sadie Murphy, telling me that Dad had gone to them as a lodger many years before and had stayed ever since. It was as if they had adopted him, which I can easily understand since he was such an easygoing, inoffensive character. They didn't have a telephone so we exchanged a few more letters. I passed the address on to my brother, John, and he got in touch too. Nick and I eventually went over to Ireland to take him out and show him his grandsons.

We found him sitting in a corner of the Murphys' front room with his newspapers, much as he had probably been for the previous twenty or more years. The Murphys had even built him his own seat in the garden so that he could read the papers in the fresh air during the summer. We took him for a drive down to Rosslare and he seemed pleased to see us in his undemonstrative way. He had no wish to talk about the past so we didn't raise the subject. He was interested to hear that Lil was still alive and still with Tom, but that was as far as it went. A few years later Bill Murphy died but Dad continued to live on peacefully with Sadie. John has been to see him more than I have since then, but I write every so often.

Nick and I moved to a lovely house in Strawberry Hill and I started to think that I would like to get back to work, having given it up when I had James. I replied to an advertisement from a local estate agent and was taken on. I bought myself a few smart business suits and got a reputation around the office for being a bit of a 'power dresser' and a career woman. I discovered I was rather good at the work and a few months later I applied to another agency for a job as a manager, not expecting to get it, but I did. Suddenly I was earning a proper salary. The owner, who was an elderly man, then sold out to the Prudential. They immediately made me a more senior manager. When the inevitable crash came at the end of the eighties I resigned and went back as a manager to my original company which had, by then, been taken over by the Abbey National.

By the beginning of the nineties Nick had grown disillusioned with the way general practice was going and decided to change career again. He had become interested in assessing physical and psychological disability and got a job as a medical adviser to the Department of Social Security. We moved out to the country and I decided I had had enough of working in an office for a while.

By this time the boys were nearly grown-up and my life in the sixties felt like a very long time ago. Now and then I used to hear something which would jolt my memories alive for a while, like the murder of John Lennon in New York. I was in my kitchen when I heard the news on the radio. It brought back all the times that I had been with Jimi when fans were mobbing him and asking for autographs. A cold-blooded murder seemed so much more shocking than the deaths of Brian, Keith and Jimi. Mike Jeffery was also dead, having been killed in an air crash. Coming back from Spain, his Iberia plane clipped wings with a jet fighter during a French air-traffic controllers' strike and everyone on board was killed.

I still stayed in touch with a lot of friends from that period and we would occasionally gossip about the old times over the phone, but on the whole I gave very little thought to it all. Then one day everything changed.

11

The seeds of what happened next were sown in 1981 when someone called and told me I should get a copy of a book called *'Scuse Me While I Kiss the Sky*, a biography of Jimi by a guy called David Henderson, which was about to come out in England. 'You'll probably be in it,' they said cheerfully.

I went to an Ealing bookshop and they managed to get me an advance copy. I certainly was in it. David Henderson was a left-wing black American civil rights activist. As I started to read it became fairly apparent that anyone white was going to be given a hard time.

When the author got round to me he gave the impression that I was permanently spaced out on acid and had been responsible for introducing Jimi to alcohol. 'Acid and alcohol,' Henderson said, 'took Jimi to another place', which I assumed he meant killed him. I felt a knot of anger tighten inside me. Not only was this completely untrue, it also seemed a very dangerous thing to say about anyone. Even if it had been true, there were a lot of people in the world who felt passionately enough about Jimi that they might decide to avenge him if they were convinced that someone was responsible for his death. And it would not have been hard for some nutter to find out where I lived.

There was more about me, and then he started to talk about Monika Danneman, the girl who had been with Jimi on the night he died. I had never heard of her until I read her name in the papers the day after Jimi died, and I still knew nothing about her eleven years later. The author was virtually accusing her of causing Jimi's death through neglect and not doing anything for him in his final hours. Both of us white women, it seemed, were guilty of corrupting Jimi and leading him to his doom.

I knew I had to do something about this book and I wondered if Monika Danneman felt the same. I decided I would try to talk to her about it, but since no one I knew had ever had any contact with her I was not sure how to set about finding her.

I decided to put a small advertisement in the *Evening Standard*, London's main daily paper, asking her to contact me at a box number. The ad appeared and a few days later I received a letter from a firm of solicitors telling me that they represented Miss Monika Danneman and that she had asked them to write to confirm that I was who I said I was in the ad. I did so, asking if she knew about the book and whether she intended to do anything about it.

Monika then made contact personally and said she would like to meet me. I invited her to our house in Ealing for a meeting with Noel and Mitch, who also wanted to talk about the book and the things it said about all of us.

Noel and Mitch arrived at the house first and we were all in the front room with the children, looking out of the window, when a taxi drew up in the road outside. All three of us stared in disbelief at the vision that emerged from the cab and paid the driver. The woman was dressed in an extraordinary pastiche of Jimi's style, even though over a decade had passed since his death and the fashions of the sixties had been relegated to the history books and were now generally regarded with ridicule. She was wearing crushed velvet bell-bottoms, a big hipster belt and a

174

sort of frilly shirt with Tom Jones sleeves. She looked like a leftover from the sixties. She was the thinnest person I had ever seen.

We chatted politely while she told us how Jimi died. As we sat round the dining table at one end of the sitting room, she took out a tape recorder and asked if she could record our conversation because her English was not very good and it would help her to be able to replay it later. 'I will make two recordings,' she promised, 'and I will give you a copy.' It didn't seem an unreasonable request if her English was that bad.

Noel, Mitch and I sat open-mouthed as she spoke, in her ponderous German accent, about the neglectful ambulance men and racist doctors who had, between them, killed Jimi. She told us how Jimi had been having trouble sleeping in her basement room at the private Samarkand Hotel in Notting Hill Gate and how she gave him some of her German sleeping pills (Vesparax). When they didn't work she gave him some more because 'they were very weak'. She said she thought he had taken about nine of the tablets in all.

She claimed that she called an ambulance when she couldn't wake him in the morning. When she was in the ambulance on the way to the hospital she had seen the paramedic sitting Jimi upright, letting his head loll forward, when he should have lain him down. When they reached the hospital, she said, the doctors ignored Jimi because he was black and he died sitting in a sort of dentist's chair. The doctor who was in charge of the case, she announced, was incompetent and racist.

Noel, Mitch and I sat in stunned silence for a while. It was a shocking story. If it was true, and we had no reason to doubt this woman's word, then there had been at worst a blatant cover-up by the authorities and at best an appallingly misman-aged inquest.

When we had finished talking as a group she asked if she and

175

I could go to the other end of the room so that she could ask me some questions about Jimi.

'Well, yeah, if you want,' I said. I did wonder what she was up to but I was distracted by the boys who had become bored of the grown-ups talking and were running around the room. I wasn't too worried. She seemed a fairly harmless eccentric. She set the tape recorder going again and started to quiz me about all sorts of personal details regarding Jimi's habits, while Noel and Mitch continued to talk at the table.

'What sort of things did Jimi like to eat? What was his favourite wine? Where did you go? What did you do together? What did you talk about?' The questions kept coming and I answered as best I could while trying to keep some sort of control over the kids. When she left we all agreed that she was one of the most bizarre people we had ever met.

I had been discovering, over the years, from people like Mitch and Noel, that Jimi had picked up some pretty weird women when he was away from home. It seemed to be almost a compulsion with him. Every night he had to have someone new and, according to the others who were on tour with him, he would often choose the worst possible dogs or crazies, take them back to his hotel room, have sex and then become agitated with them and ask them to leave. I had witnessed something of this with Angie and the other girl – although they were certainly no dogs – at the Londonderry. There was even an incident Noel told me about where Jimi hit a girl with a brick. Perhaps he was avenging himself on women in some way, or perhaps there are lots of men who would behave like that if they had had the same opportunities or disappointments as Jimi. The story reinforced my belief that Jimi had changed completely towards the end of his life. He seemed to be losing control, becoming angry, frustrated and bad-tempered.

We assumed that Monika was just one more of these casual

Nick Page

Me with Lenny Kravitz – a whole new generation

Night before the Blue Plaque *(clockwise)*: Amir Amirani (film-maker of the event), Clare Goldstein, Nick, Noel, Gerry Goldstein (who filmed us in the sixties), me and Candace

Pete Townshend gives his speech; I receive flowers from the McCartneys (who couldn't be there); Francis Carnwath, Chairman of the Blue Plaque Committee, looks on *(courtesy of Chris Taylor/*Mojo*)*

(Below) Me, a champagne bucket given to me by the fans – and is that marijuana in the background? *(courtesy of Hey Joers)*

(Above) The blue plaque party *(clockwise)*: Mike Avory (Kinks), Tim Rose, Anna Capaldi, me, John Paul Jones (Led Zeppelin), Dave Rowberry (Animals); *(on floor)* Jim Capaldi (Traffic), Madeline Bell *(courtesy of Chris Taylor/*Mojo*)*

(Above) The blue plaque at Brook Street, with friends – Noel, Pete and me

'Wonderful to see you again, my friend' – Zoot Money *(courtesy of Chris Taylor/*Mojo*)*

Rolan Bolan, me and Madeline *(courtesy of Chris Taylor/*Mojo*)*

groupies, who had had the misfortune to be there on the night everything went wrong. It was unclear whether she intended to try to stop the book which I had contacted her about, but I had decided to go ahead on my own anyway. She wasn't someone who inspired me with confidence, so I hadn't suggested any sort of joint action.

As she was saying goodbye, she had issued an open invitation for us to visit her at her home in Seaford on the South Coast. It so happened that Nick's grandparents lived near there, so the next time we were visiting them we phoned her and she invited us round for a cup of tea. As we walked into her house the alarm bells began to ring. Monika, it appeared, had set herself up as the keeper of the Hendrix shrine. Every wall was covered with paintings of Jimi which, Monika informed us, she had done herself.

At one stage she started talking about some tablets which the doctor kept telling her to take but which she didn't want. She showed them to Nick and asked him about them. He told her that she should do whatever her doctor suggested and acted as if he didn't know anything about them. I could see they were a major tranquillizer.

Nick got chatting to her for a while and then said that we had to go but that we would keep in touch.

'Give me a ring any time,' she said in her doleful monotone, 'but don't phone me on a full moon. On the full moon Jimi and I are in communication. We go together travelling on the astral plane.'

'OK, Monika, we'll remember that,' he said and we made our move, heading down the garden path as fast as was seemly.

Having decided that whatever I was going to do about this book I would have to do on my own, I went to my lawyers and told them that I wanted the piece about my leading Jimi to his death with drink and drugs taken out before the book was published. The lawyers managed to stop publication in Britain and when the book reappeared ten years later the piece about me was gone, but the material about Monika was still there.

Meanwhile Monika had contacted the press, telling them that the reason the book was delayed was because she had stopped publication due to the things the author had said about her. It was annoying that she was telling a blatant untruth, but it didn't seem worth following up since we had already decided that she was rather out of touch with reality. It looked to me as if we had managed to deal with the problem and I could return to my post-Hendrix life without any more dramas. Which is what I did, until exactly ten years later.

Nick and I were getting ready to go out to dinner when Noel Redding rang from his home in Ireland. I could tell immediately that he was in a terrible state and in tears. 'Can you help me,' he wanted to know, 'I've been served a writ by Monika Danneman.'

'What for?' I asked.

'Well,' he explained, 'you know I've written a book. I said that after Jimi was sick on the night he died, Monika went out for cigarettes. The writ says I'm accusing her of negligence.'

'I don't know what I can do,' I said, 'but let me think about it and come back to you.'

That evening I remembered Dee, Mitch Mitchell's girlfriend, who I had met briefly a couple of weeks before when Mitch had launched his book (books on the sixties seemed to be coming out every few minutes at that time) at the Hard Rock Café in London. Dee had sent me an invitation out of the blue and, since I hadn't seen Mitch in years, I had decided to go down there to see him and any other old faces that might turn up. Dee told me her name was Diana Bonham-Carter and that she was a member of the famous family of British aristocrats. She was a very entertaining and witty character and one of the things she had told me was that she had once been a BBC researcher.

It occurred to me that she might be a good person to do some digging into what had really happened after Jimi's death. Perhaps she could find the ambulance men and doctors who were on duty that day and ask them to clarify things. I wanted to help Noel so I asked her if she thought she could do anything.

'Well, I don't really get on very well with Noel,' she told me, 'but I would be happy to try to help.' She was true to her word and a week or so later she came back to me having tracked down the ambulance drivers, who, in over twenty years, had never ever been interviewed or spoken to about the events of that morning.

'I started at the ambulance station for the area,' she explained, 'and they sent me to their retirement association. Someone there remembered who one of them was, Reg Jones, and I rang him.'

He said he remembered the case. 'But when we got there the bloke was already dead. He didn't die in the ambulance,' he explained.

Dee asked him nicely if we could take him out to lunch to talk about it some more, and he readily agreed.

Since Dee didn't have a car I arranged to pick Reg up and then take him to meet Dee in a pub we knew in Holland Park. He seemed rather nervy when I got there but pleased to be invited out. His wife had died recently and he was living alone with his poodle. All the way there he seemed to think he was back in his ambulance, issuing instructions to his driver and giving a non-stop running commentary on the road conditions: 'There's a lorry coming up on your right-hand side, there's a woman crossing the road fifty yards ahead, there's a corner coming up and a car turning right; traffic lights ahead, they're changing to red . . .'

When we finally drew up in front of the pub he gave a satisfied nod and said, 'Well, for a woman you're not a bad driver.'

Once we got settled, Reg told us his story. 'When we got to the flat the door was wide open. The body was on the bed, covered in vomit of all colours, black, brown; all over him, all over the pillow. There wasn't another soul in sight. I went back to the ambulance for an aspirator. We tried to revive him but we couldn't. The vomit was all dried, like he'd been lying there a long time. There was no heartbeat. He was blue, not breathing and not responding to light or pain. We called the police from the radio in the ambulance, thinking he was dead and that the circumstances were strange. A couple of young policemen turned up and they told us to take him to the hospital.'

'Is that the normal procedure?' I asked.

'No. Strictly speaking they shouldn't have done that but they didn't want to have to spend the whole afternoon filling in forms. We helped them out by taking the deceased to the casualty department. None of us realized it was Jimi Hendrix until we read it in the newspapers later that day.'

What the policemen should have done if they found a dead body was call in the CID, but as far as they were concerned this was just another dead junkie in Notting Hill. Had Jimi been in the Cumberland Hotel where everyone knew who he was, it would have been a different story.

Reg's account completely contradicted everything that Monika had been telling people. She said she rode in the ambulance with Jimi and that he was still alive. Reg claimed that there was no one else at the scene, that no one came with them in the ambulance and that Jimi was already dead when they turned up. We really needed to find the other ambulance man to see if his story was the same or if Reg's memory had become clouded with time. Unfortunately Reg could only remember that it wasn't his usual partner working with him that day, and he thought the man's name was an unusual one like Sual.

Dee went back to her contact at the retirement association

and told him about Sual. He got back to her almost straight away. 'I've had another look at my book,' he said, 'and the bloke's name was Suau.'

Directory Enquiries told us there was only one person with that name in London, who turned out to be the ambulance man's father. I gave him a ring. 'My son lives in Ashby de la Zouch now,' he told us, 'I'll give you his number.'

Dee rang him, with me listening in on the extension, and asked him all the same questions we had asked Reg. His answers were exactly the same. He corroborated his partner's story completely. At the end of the conversation Dee said, 'Don't you remember the blonde girl who was there? She had long, silver-blonde hair and a German accent.' There was an extended silence and then he said, 'Doesn't ring any bells. I don't remember there being anyone there.'

We were now sure that Monika's version of the story had been adapted to suit her needs, but we felt we needed to gather as much evidence as possible for Noel before confronting her lawyers. The myth of Jimi's death which had been more or less accepted for over twenty years was beginning to unravel before our eyes.

The next thing we tried to do was find the policemen who had attended the scene, which proved to be difficult. Eventually we heard that one of them, who was now a publican in Aylesbury, had been talking to a rock journalist about that morning in Notting Hill. We went up on the train to see him and his story fitted exactly with the other two: Jimi was dead when he got to the hotel. He thought he was with another policeman but couldn't remember who he was.

Donald Teare, the man who had actually done the autopsy on Jimi, was dead so we needed to talk to another expert. Dr Rufus Crompton, Director of Forensic Medicine at St George's Medical School had worked with Professor Teare. We gave him a copy of the autopsy report and asked how, in his opinion, Jimi had died.

'He would have died from the amount of sleeping pills he had taken anyway,' he told us. 'The fact that he vomited and inhaled the vomit just hastened it. The reading in his liver was so high he couldn't have survived it. He couldn't have been breathing by the time he reached the hospital because his lungs were full of fluid, half a pint in one of them. What makes you think he took nine of these tablets?'

'The girl who was with him said that's what happened,' we explained.

'Well,' the doctor looked doubtful, 'I would say you wouldn't need more than about five of those tablets to get this reading but I'll ask a toxicologist what the dose could have been.' Dee told me the toxicologist said that it was impossible to say. It could have been as few as four tablets or as many as nine.

Suddenly the picture had changed again. Instead of the image of the irresponsible rock star knocking back handfuls of pills, which the media had been happy to run with and build on, it seemed that he might have taken just a few. Monika had said that the tablets were very weak. If this was what she told Jimi he could have taken four or five just to get to sleep.

I knew that Eric Burdon had written about the morning of Jimi's death in his autobiography. Ronnie Money had given me her copy of the book when I visited her once and so I looked it out and read it again. He wrote that Jimi had been jamming with him at Ronnie Scott's club in Frith Street the night before (in fact it may have been a couple of nights before). Eric claimed that Monika had rung him and his girlfriend Alvinia, very early in the morning, saying that Jimi was so stoned she couldn't wake him up. Eric suggested hot coffee and a slap round the face and went back to sleep. As he dozed, alarm bells started going in his head and he rang Monika back, telling her to call an ambulance quickly. She protested that she couldn't because there were drugs in the flat. He told her to get rid of them but to get help fast. He promised to come over as quickly as he could, Alvinia going on ahead. He said he got to the flat just as the ambulance was leaving and that Alvinia and Monika were both crying. I phoned Eric to ask him more, recording the conversation so that I could play it back to Dee.

'Well,' I said, 'what happened that morning, Eric? Where was Jimi when you got there?'

'I think I saw Jimi on the bed,' he admitted, 'but I couldn't look because of the mess.' He told me that he and Terry the Pill, his road manager, tried to clean the flat up so that when the ambulance arrived they wouldn't find any incriminating evidence. At some later stage Gerry Stickells went down there as well. The more we found out, the more Jimi's death looked like a black farce with all these people rushing around trying to cover up for a man who was almost certainly dead.

What I couldn't work out was why there was a gap between Monika and Eric talking on the phone at about six or six-thirty in the morning and the ambulance actually being called at eleven-eighteen. What had Monika been doing in the intervening hours? She admitted she went out for cigarettes, but that wouldn't have taken long.

Nothing that happened that morning, it was turning out, was anything like the version the authorities had accepted as being true, and it seemed to me that we had enough evidence to warrant a reopening of the inquest. I compiled a file and sent it to the Attorney General, pointing out that at the original inquest they had all been happy to take Monika's word for what happened, but that the people who were there on the morning in question told a completely different story. I explained that Monika was saying the ambulance men and doctors were responsible for his death and that if that was so, an official complaint should be lodged against them. Among other things I wanted to clear these people's names. I didn't like the idea of the health service being seen in the eyes of the world to have killed off Jimi Hendrix through negligence, when clearly that was not the case.

I wanted Monika to be made to substantiate her accusations. The Attorney General instructed the Crown Prosecution Service to pass the file to Scotland Yard's Special Operations 1 (SO1). The first man I talked to there was Detective Superintendent Douglas Campbell, who phoned me. He sounded like a fatherly man. He made an appointment to come and see me. We went to the pub together to discuss everything and got on very well. I liked him. An insider must have leaked the story to the press because a few days later it was all over the papers and they started printing some wild guesses at what was going on.

We had wanted to keep quiet the fact that Angie was dead as she was at the party on Jimi's final night and would have been a key witness. If Monika knew she was no longer around to testify she would feel a lot more comfortable. When the press went to Chas Chandler, however, he knew nothing about this and happily told them about Angie's death. The press printed it and Superintendent Campbell thought I had given the game away. He phoned me and I could tell that he was very angry. The next day he found out what had really happened but I was upset that he thought it was me that had told the press.

Superintendent Campbell was nearing retirement and didn't fancy hauling over to America to interrogate people like Eric, so he asked the FBI to do it for him, but when the FBI knocked on Eric's door he didn't want to talk to them. I think if the English officers had gone over in person they would have been more successful. They were not the sort of men to take no for an answer. Special Operations One officers were the oddest policemen I have ever met. They were the Overseas and International Crime Investigation Branch. Superintendent Campbell drove around in what appeared to be an ordinary Volkswagen but which was obviously souped-up, with a number of odd-looking radio aerials. His men looked like giant rugby players with broken noses and cauliflower ears, but some had degrees in history and psychology and could speak Spanish, Arabic and Russian. If they didn't frighten international organized criminals they certainly frightened me.

When she heard what was going on Monika went ape, one moment welcoming the investigation and claiming that she had always thought there was something suspicious about the way Jimi died, the next saying that she was being accused of lying and that I was trying to reinvent Jimi's death. 'Why,' she wanted to know, 'has Kathy decided to speak up now after remaining silent for over twenty years?'

Although Eric and Alvinia wouldn't speak to the police and Gerry Stickells refused to add anything to his previous statements, Terry the Pill gave a statement confirming that he had gone down to the flat and hidden drugs in the garden. He told the investigators that he arrived just as the ambulance was leaving, although he told me before the investigation that when he got there Jimi was lying on the bed, 'knackered'. He also told the police that after the ambulance left Monika was still there with him, which completely contradicted her story that she was in the ambulance witnessing Jimi being mishandled by the ambulance men.

The SO1 men suggested that Monika had got the idea of Jimi's being made to sit up after watching him from outside the hotel being carried up the steps from the basement in a special chair because the climb was too steep for a stretcher, but once he was inside the ambulance he would have been laid out flat. The ambulance men, however, had no memory of her being there at all.

The investigators came to the conclusion that the ambulance men and the doctors were not guilty of anything, that Jimi was certainly dead by the time he arrived at the hospital and probably before he was put into the ambulance. They told me that they thought Monika was barking mad, but that she had her story so well worked out after twenty years they couldn't do much about it. The two main witnesses they wanted to interview were Eric and Alvinia but they were both in the US and the FBI hadn't managed to speak to them. One of the policemen told me that he thought all the witnesses were 'f—ing lying' for different reasons of their own.

When the enquiry was concluded Monika announced to the press that she had been completely vindicated by it, which was odd, as in fact it did the opposite, vindicating all the people she had accused of killing Jimi.

When her case against Noel came to court the judge threw it out, accusing her of being paranoid and vexatious. Just because Noel had written that she had gone out to buy cigarettes after Jimi vomited didn't mean he was saying she was negligent in any way. That should have been the end of the whole thing, but Monika hadn't finished. It seemed she was determined to keep after me.

We were in Noel's place in Ireland for New Year's Eve at the beginning of 1995 when Tom rang to say that Lil was seriously ill.

As soon as we got back to England I drove straight to the Countess of Chester Hospital. I found her in a private room, presumably put there because they thought she was going to die. Tom was sitting quietly in a corner of the room.

'Hallo, Mum,' I said, 'it's me.'

'Oh hallo, Jean,' she said.

'It's not Jean,' I said, 'it's Kathleen.'

'Kathleen? Ooh, I haven't seen her for a long time.'

'No, it's me, Kathleen.'

'Oh,' she peered at me again, 'oh yes. It's nice to see you Kathleen. I suppose you've come because I'm dying.'

'Don't be so silly,' I said, 'of course you're not dying.'

'Yes you are,' Tom chirped up from his corner.

'Who's that over there?' she wanted to know, 'is that Mam?'

'It's just the hospital gown hanging behind the door,' I explained.

'When all this is over,' she said, 'I'm going to have a good holiday.'

'Where would you like to go then?' I asked. 'Would you like to go back to Rhyl?'

'Oh no,' she said, 'anywhere but Rhyl. I'd like to go in a caravan somewhere.'

I decided that I had better go and talk to the doctor in charge. He was a young ginger-haired Scotsman. 'What's going to happen?' I asked, 'is her leg going gangrenous? Are you thinking of amputation?'

'Yes, we are thinking of it.'

'What are the chances of her surviving that sort of operation?'

'Well,' he said, 'all operations are dodgy when you get to seventy-five.'

'Seventy-five!' I was shocked. 'She's ninety.'

Momentarily covered in confusion, he looked at his notes. 'I've got seventy-five here.'

'Well,' I said, 'I hope this won't change the way you treat her, but she's certainly a lot older than that.'

I went back in to talk to her again. 'Would you like a beer, Mum?'

'Oh yes, I'd like a Mackeson.'

I sent Tom to buy one and she began to perk up. They even put her back on the ward and after a few more days I went back to Nick and the boys. I was beginning to think that I would have to find her an old people's home. I was also feeling guilty about giving away her age because they then dropped the idea of operating on her. Nick consoled me, saying that, just like her mother before her, she would never have survived the anaesthetic.

A few weeks later Tom rang to tell us she had died suddenly. I was shocked even though it had been coming for so long. 'What happened?'

'She started making funny noises,' I could tell that he was having trouble holding back the tears, 'and then she sat up and said, "I'm going to die, Tom," and those were her last words.'

At the funeral we kept the lie about her age going to the end.

12

During our investigations Dee had shown me a copy of a manuscript which Monika had written and sent to an American writer, telling of her 'life' with Jimi. Presumably she was hoping to find a publisher as Mitch and Noel had. In it she said that Jimi had told her to beware of me because I cheated and lied for money and had stolen all of his belongings. The whole manuscript was laughable, written in English with Germanic grammar and sentence construction and full of fantasies and mystical ramblings. She even claimed that Jimi had told her Al wasn't his real father, which was ridiculous.

I thought it highly unlikely that she would ever find a reputable publisher and, although it was unpleasant to see such lies about oneself in black and white, I might have let it go by had I not discovered that she had been repeating the accusations against me to an author called Tony Brown who was preparing another book on Jimi.

I had no way of knowing how many other people were being told these things. At the time I couldn't understand why she was doing this, but gradually it dawned on me that she wanted to discredit me so that she could build up her role as Jimi's one great love and fiancée.

I had heard that she had been quoted as telling journalists the things I had told her about at our first meeting in the sitting room in Ealing, which she had taped. She was passing off as her own the information I had given her about Jimi's private habits. I decided I had to take action to stop her from spreading any more nonsense about me. If I didn't make a stand at this stage there was no telling what she would do next, so I went back to my lawyers.

Her only line of defence was that she hadn't written the manuscript and she blamed the American writer she had sent it to, even though it was quite apparent that the words had come from someone who did not speak English very well, not from an educated American. When her lawyers realized we weren't buying that story they agreed to settle out of court, giving me an apology and an undertaking that Monika would not continue saying nasty things about me, plus £1,000 as token damages and costs. All I wanted was for her to stop this nonsense. I thought the injunction would take care of it. That, I thought, would be the end of it all.

Monika, however, had more than one manuscript up her sleeve. She had actually written six different manuscripts and in the autumn of 1995 she managed to get Bloomsbury to publish a book called *The Inner World of Jimi Hendrix*, which made official her claim that she and Jimi were engaged (she even got Jimi's father to believe and confirm it, but then he knew virtually nothing about his son's private life after he left home as a teenager).

The first I heard of the book was from Martin Shankleman, a BBC reporter doing a radio programme, 'In the Wink of an Eye', about the last days of Jimi Hendrix. Martin had first rung me a few months before, asking for an interview. He had already been to see Monika by that stage and had heard her side of the story. I could tell he was treating anything I said with some suspicion, believing that my main objective was to be vindictive towards Monika, inventing stories to discredit her. So I gave him the telephone numbers of all the people who had told Dee and me their accounts of Jimi's death. A few days later he came back having spoken to each of them and realized that Monika had been weaving a fantasy for him. He interviewed them for the programme and they repeated their stories exactly as we had heard them. It was becoming increasingly hard for Monika to find people who would believe her, leaving only the more obsessive and blinkered Hendrix fans to follow her mystic tales about Jimi's supernatural powers.

'Have you seen Monika's book?' Martin asked me during the course of one of our later conversations.

'What book?'

'She's publishing an autobiography. You should see what she says about you in the last pages.'

'Oh,' my heart sank, 'can you fax them to me?'

'No,' he laughed, 'I'm not going to fax them to you.'

'Why not?'

'I'm not going to be responsible for republishing what she says. I'll read it to you but I'm not going to send it.'

He proceeded to read the offending passages down the line. Basically Monika was saying that I had lied to the Attorney General and made accusations against her which were unfounded and that she had been vindicated in every way by the resulting investigation. I was now really furious and rang a rock magazine which I was told had reviewed the book (saying it was a load of crap) and asked if they had a copy. They had and agreed to fax the offending pages to me. I read it and was dismayed once more, but I decided not to go to law again at that stage. The sheer hassle of it all, not to mention the costs, didn't seem worth it. I reasoned that no one would take any notice: everyone would realize they were the ramblings of a madwoman and that soon it would all be water under the bridge.

Then I received a call from Bob Doerschuk who had just

taken over as editor of *Musician* magazine in America and was looking for a big scoop. He had heard what was going on about Monika from another rock journalist and he wanted to follow it up. He asked if I would be willing to talk about it and I agreed. He said he would come over to England and check out everything himself. The magazine's lawyers were insistent that he get everything right so that Monika was left with absolutely no grounds to sue them.

Bob arrived in England, staying in a local hotel for about five days and listening to the whole story again. I told him everything I knew and gave him all the paperwork. He then spent several weeks doing follow-up research, refusing to put anything into the article until it had been checked. Everything he discovered contradicted Monika's stories. He interviewed Philip Harvey who had been with her and Jimi the night before and had seen that they were not a loving couple, as she claimed. She appeared to be more of an employee of Jimi's than a girlfriend, according to Philip's description. He said she became irrationally jealous of the other women Jimi talked to on his last evening and that they had had a huge row in the street outside his mews house.

Not only did he expose her account of the final hours of Jimi's life, but also her claims that they were engaged, or that they even had a relationship beyond that of a star and his casual groupie. They had met once many years before and had met again just a few days before Jimi died. The resulting article was published as the magazine's cover story in February 1996 and Monika was furious. One of her friends rang Bob in America and he called to tell me about it.

'The caller says she doesn't know you,' Bob told me over the phone, 'but Monika has told her that you married the doctor who saved your life after you were found in the street having taken a heroin overdose. She said you were a bit of a party girl then and you're still a party girl now.'

That was when I reached the end of my tether. It was bad enough when she attacked me, but when she started involving my family I was no longer willing to stay quiet. I wasn't going to be branded by a loony as a hopeless junkie. I wasn't going to have Nick and the boys subjected to such insults. Not only was Monika now blatantly ignoring the legal undertaking she had made not to go round telling lies about me, she actually seemed to be inventing new ones. What I didn't realize was that someone else was feeding her the lies and that she was just repeating them. No matter how much hassle and cost it might involve, I had to put an end to all the rumours about me. I headed back to the lawyers and they served her with a contempt of court notification.

The Monika Danneman publicity machine went into top gear in the intervening period with a huge spread in *Hello* magazine showing her with Al Hendrix and other members of his family supporting her at the graveside as Jimi's grieving fiancée. She had already had six pages of coverage in the same magazine about eighteen months before, showing her working on her pictures of Hendrix at her home and telling how she had been vindicated in the police inquiry.

Two days before we went to court we offered her an olive branch via her lawyers, saying that we didn't want to take her to court, we just wanted her to abide by her undertaking and agree to stop repeating the accusations against me. They wrote back rejecting the offer and saying that it showed the weakness of our case and they would see us in court. We later discovered that the same firm of lawyers had represented her at Jimi's inquest, which was mystifying. Why would she have felt she needed legal representation at something as straightforward as an inquiry into cause of death?

When we got to the courtroom Monika was wearing a hairy electric-blue coat, scarlet satin shirt, chunky, dangling necklaces and earrings and long snake rings on all her fingers. Her long hair was peroxide blonde and her face was plastered in make-up.

The judge seemed unimpressed by the fact that she arrived in his courtroom with a pile of her books, big coffee-table style publications full of her psychedelic paintings of Jimi, accompanied by eccentric ramblings about spiritual forces and messages, which she then proceeded to distribute.

Monika was accompanied by a tanned young man with a cockney accent who appeared to have some sort of public relations function, and who told the press that I had been conducting a twenty-six-year feud with Monika and that I had asked the judge to jail her, which was certainly not the case. In fact we had asked the judge twice not to give her a jail sentence, which could follow conviction for contempt of court, and that she should simply be made to follow the injunction.

At the beginning of the proceedings she actually gave one of her books to the judge, at which point my QC leant forward and muttered, *sotto voce*: 'Mistake number one.'

Monika seemed totally certain that everything she was saying was true, even though she couldn't produce a single piece of evidence to substantiate any of her accusations against me. She had not been informed of the evidence gathered by the police and it became increasingly obvious to everyone in the room that she was not in a balanced state of mind. Her lawyers actually gave up trying to claim that what she had said about me was the truth, saying instead that she was just trying to defend herself against me. The judge, however, saw quite clearly that it was the other way round, and that it was I who was being persecuted by her.

'Miss Etchingham,' it was pointed out, 'has never actually done or said anything against Miss Danneman.'

He found her guilty of contempt of court, applying the criminal standard of proof 'beyond reasonable doubt'.

When the judgement came down in our favour we were all very relieved and leapt up from our seats to congratulate one another. Going to law is always a risk, and highly stressful. We went out into the hallway, talking happily, and Monika staggered past us as if she were drunk. It was as if she didn't know where she was going.

'Is she on tranquillizers, do you think?' I asked Nick.

'No,' he shook his head, 'I think she's just shocked.'

As she headed towards the fire exit like a zombie her lawyers intercepted her and turned her round, pointing her in the right direction. She then went home to her mother.

The next day the press said that in court I had looked as if I was in control whereas Monika had cut a sad figure: 'a superannuated rock chick'. I thought that was rather cruel but I was surprised her lawyers hadn't advised her to present herself better for a High Court appearance.

According to the newspapers on the following day, Monika's neighbours said they saw her pottering around in her garden. She was probably collecting up the two lengths of hosepipe with which she killed herself that night.

Once her mother was in bed she went out to the garage, carefully closing the door behind her. She fixed the two pieces of hosepipe to the twin exhausts of her new Mercedes and fed them in through the front windows of the car. Then she taped up the gaps at the top of the windows, climbed into the driving seat and started the car. Just as she was about to lose consciousness she switched off the engine so that the noise didn't attract attention. She must have been serious about wanting to end her life. Perhaps she believed that she would be able to join Jimi wherever he had gone.

I knew that as soon as the news got on to Reuters and the Press Association the house would be besieged with reporters, so I quickly prepared a statement saying how shocked and saddened I was to hear of Monika's death and that I held no personal animosity towards her and felt nothing but great sympathy for her family. By the time I got back with the shopping for the weekend the drive was packed. I read my statement from the front steps.

On Sunday the telephone rang and I picked it up. 'Is that Kathy Etchingham?' a woman asked.

'Yes.'

'I just want you to know,' she shrieked, 'that as far as we're concerned you're a murderer.' She hung up. I guessed who she was because several of Monika's friends had rung in the past posing as reporters to try to get me to say something derogatory about her so she could sue me. I never fell for it: I could always hear them turning on their tape machines. I dialled 1471 and found the caller's number. We waited an hour and then Nick rang and asked to speak to her.

'Any more phone calls like that and I'll call the police,' he said calmly and hung up. Luckily Nick's parents were there for the Easter weekend and they helped by being very matter-of-fact about it.

'The woman was obviously barmy,' they said. 'It was a pity that her friends and family humoured her fantasies instead of trying to get her sorted out.'

I still felt terribly sorry for the woman. She had constructed an elaborate fantasy about her relationship with Jimi to protect herself from the truth about the night he died, and slowly the whole thing had crumbled and finally collapsed.

We didn't hear from Monika's shrieking friend again but another of her supporters posted a letter on the 'Hey Joe' mailing list on the Internet calling me a prostitute and a murderer. There was nothing we could do to trace the letter but I had now recovered enough to ignore it.

The following month Noel was doing a book signing in New

York when a man called Al Romero, claiming to be an old friend of Monika's, burst into Virgin Megastore and started shouting that Monika had told him I was a murderer, a rapist and a child abuser, and the security guards had to throw him out.

What I didn't realize was that at the time someone had fed Monika these lies, letting her do the dirty work on their behalf. I was soon to find out who.

I don't think there is any business that attracts so many fantasists, conmen and flakes as the music business. As if there weren't enough of them actually working in the industry, there are all the others who are attracted to the scene who have to invent roles for themselves. Some of them do it by providing sexual services, some just hang around until someone offers them a job so that they can call themselves 'personal assistants' or 'roadies'. Some just nominate themselves as 'a close friend' of a star, while others provide drugs. Perhaps it is the music that first attracts them, or the sexual imagery that the business projects. Perhaps it is simply the fame, or the easy access to other people's drugs and money. Whatever it is, there are none stranger than the sad cases still living in the shadow of the sixties.

Although I found Dee entertaining company, I was always aware that she could be a little unpredictable. She seemed to be totally involved in the music scene. The first time I had seen her act truly bizarrely was in New York when we went to a music awards dinner together. On the way there in the limo she told me that Noel's girlfriend, Candace, had hired some Puerto Rican women to beat her up in the ladies' loo. I dismissed the suggestion as ridiculous since it was a private party with guests like Neil Young and Phil Spector attending.

When Candy, who I had never met before, arrived with Noel at the venue Dee flew into the most extraordinary tirade against her. It should have been a warning to me but I have always had a short memory when it comes to other people's bad behaviour,

197

and Dee swept me along with the sheer power of her personality. I heard odd stories about her from various people, but I never gave them much credence.

After we had worked together so effectively on finding out about the night Jimi died, we had remained very friendly. She would often call me at home just to chat. But, gradually, the calls increased in regularity until eventually she was ringing several times a day. Nick was beginning to get annoyed, with the phone going constantly from morning till evening.

'She's lonely,' I defended, 'with Mitch out all the time. She doesn't have a car or anything.' But I had to agree that it was becoming a bit obsessive. If ever she didn't call for a few days she would always have some grand excuse, like she had been staying with some of her aristocratic Bonham-Carter relations. I was beginning to suspect that the stories she was telling weren't true. In one of these calls she told me she had been in Geneva looking at a flat she and Mitch were thinking of buying, as they needed to leave the UK to avoid huge tax bills.

'You can't just go and live in Geneva,' I said innocently, 'they don't let people just go and live there.'

'What do you know?' she snapped, 'what do you know?' and hung up.

She had always told me that her father had been an ambassador in the US, which was why she had a slight American accent. Nick's father, however, had worked with diplomats all his life and he said that there had never been a Bonham-Carter in Washington. 'As far as I know,' he said, 'none of the Bonham-Carters were ever in the diplomatic service.'

She also told us that she had attended St Mary's, a well-known Catholic girls' school in Ascot. We knew a family of girls who had been there over the same period and none of them had ever heard of her. Warning bells began to ring in my mind but Dee was very plausible and amusing, so I ignored them.

Sometimes when she was on the phone she would suddenly have to go, 'because someone is looking through the window'. She would then ring back, claiming that the neighbours were always peering in, in the hope of catching a glimpse of Mitch, 'because he's such a big star'. Looking back now it seems obvious that her behaviour was unusual, but when you are actually dealing with people like Dee on a day-to-day basis they are very good at making the things they say seem normal. I was also distracted by my troubles with Monika.

Then Dee developed a habit of standing behind me and fiddling absent-mindedly with my hair. Part of me was aware that there might be some sexual vibrations in the air but I have always worked on the theory that if you ignore these things they usually go away. I did, however, realize that something had to be done when I was staying with her on one occasion when Mitch was away and she came into my bedroom stark naked at six o'clock in the morning, claiming to be looking for a book. When I dashed into the loo she followed and started taking a shower, saying breezily, 'Don't take any notice of me.'

The alarms were now going off overtime and I cooled the relationship right down. I could tell she was slightly offended but it didn't seem too bad. Then we started to get telephone calls at all hours of the day and night, the caller either hanging up when we answered or making strange noises like the rustling of paper. One night we received a call from Nick's brother.

'I thought you ought to know,' he said, 'the police have been making enquiries about you.'

'What sort of enquiries?'

'About drug dealing.'

Apparently two young plain-clothes officers had been around to see his brother's ex-sister-in-law. They said that someone had informed them that Nick had been struck off the medical register and was selling drugs.

When I told Nick this latest piece of news we decided to go down to the police station and find out what was going on. We requested to speak to the Inspector.

'I know nothing about this,' he said. 'The detective in charge of these two officers is not in today but I'll try to confirm whether an investigation is going on and let you know.'

'If they are making investigations about me being struck off the medical register,' Nick said, as calmly as he could manage, 'wouldn't it be better to go to the General Medical Council first, rather than my brother's ex-sister-in-law?'

We could see that the Inspector was feeling uncomfortable but he obviously didn't know what was going on, so we agreed to wait to hear from him. Before going, however, we did tell him about Dee, how she seemed to have become obsessed with me and that she was known for doing vicious things to people. I would imagine that the moment we left the station they rang the General Medical Council and discovered that not only had Nick not been struck off, but that he was a civil servant and part of a team that advised a minister. I would also imagine that at that stage the investigation was taken out of the hands of the two overzealous and incautious young policemen who had taken Dee's call and given to a more senior officer.

After the weekend the Detective Inspector in charge of the case came round and we told him the whole story. 'Basically,' Nick summed up for me, 'this woman is stalking my wife.' The mist suddenly seemed to clear before the officer's eyes and he understood what we were trying to tell him. He reddened and started to fiddle with his tie.

'I see,' he said. 'What we've got here is a vicious dyke!'

Just as we had been unravelling Monika's lies, we now started to discover that Dee had been busy behind the scenes as well. It emerged that she had also given the police the name of Tony Brown, the author and Jimi Hendrix archivist, as another person who would confirm that I was a dope dealer and they had been to interview him, asking if I had ever supplied him with drugs.

Brown was astonished, and refuted the suggestion.

She had also phoned the social services and informed them that I was abusing my children. The police asked to meet the boys, who were home from school on holiday, and were a little taken aback when they saw the size of them. I pointed out that they were both at boarding school and a call to their headmaster would ascertain whether they had been exhibiting any signs of abuse. They spoke to James and he laughingly told them that if anybody abused anybody in the family it was him 'abusing' me, not the other way round! At that stage the police became convinced that not only was their time being wasted, they were also being put in a potentially embarrassing position. Dee's lying had been so masterful that she had convinced every person she had spoken to of the truth of her accusations. We were all equally anxious to put a stop to her campaign.

When the police left the house they said they would deal with the matter in their own way. A third party informed us that an hour and a quarter later they raided Dee's house in Rye and strongly advised her not to waste any more police time.

We discovered that she was continuing to spread rumours about us on the telephone to New York, and so we went to the Medical Defence Union. We explained that I was being harassed and stalked by an impostor posing as an English woman. The last time we had to ask them for help was when a woman had become obsessed with Nick and started stalking him. They must have thought we had this sort of trouble all the time. They sent Dee a threatening lawyer's letter and within a few days we heard that she and Mitch had moved to France. The police investigations revealed that she wasn't who she said she was, but they weren't permitted to reveal her real identity.

Once she was on French soil, we later discovered, she started communicating with Monika, telling her that I was the worst person in the world and encouraging her to expose me in her book. Dee fed Monika with all the false information she put into her book, promising to support her should I try to sue. Monika's lawyers must have taken the worst bits out but not all of them. Of course when the time came for Monika to defend her words in court Dee had vanished and poor Monika was left to face the music alone.

Once we started asking around about Dee's activities we discovered that she had developed obsessions about other people connected with Jimi, including Noel Redding. She had actually moved over to Ireland to be near him and had attacked him in the street, nearly ruining his seventeen-year relationship with his girlfriend of the time, Carol. When Carol was killed in a car crash Dee thought she had a chance and was consumed with jealousy when he started dating Candy, a make-up artist at NBC. She rang Candy's boss on the Letterman Show, telling him that she was Mitch Mitchell's agent and she was going to sue the company because Candy had been overheard at a BBC cocktail party saying that Mitch was a drunk and a drug addict. Candy nearly lost her job before she was able to prove that she wasn't even in England at the time.

Suddenly I understood what the row had been about at the dinner in New York (an incident Dee had turned on its head by telling people that it was me who had attacked Candy, not her). At the time I hadn't known about her crush on Noel.

When she was working for former model Celia Hammond's cat charity Dee had caused similar problems for Celia. The more people we talked to, the more horror stories we heard.

She had once told me about a record producer she knew and I mentioned his name to Candy. By this time I was keen to find out as much about Dee's background as possible. Candy knew the man and gave him a call. He laughed and said he knew all about Dee. She used to be married to an English musician called Robin Clayton, and was 'obsessed with anyone who comes from the sixties scene in London. She's the world's biggest liar.'

From him we traced Robin Clayton to an address in Fulham. 'Do you know somebody called Dee?' I asked the man who answered the door.

'Oh,' he moaned, 'you'd better come in. Now what's she done?'

We told him the whole story and he listened in unsurprised silence. 'Well,' he said eventually, 'she has obviously got worse but she was always a liar. I met her when she was a cocktail waitress in Cambridge, Massachusetts. Her name was Dolores Cullen. I married her and brought her back to England. The moment we got here she divorced me.' He insisted on showing me a group photo and asked me to point her out in case it wasn't the same person. I had no trouble. We both knew now.

'Where does she come from?' I asked, confused.

'Cleveland, Ohio. She's American, didn't you know? She was obsessed with the British rock scene and worked on speaking with an English accent. My mother gave her £1,500 to go back to America, but she never went. The last time I saw her,' he said, 'she was walking down the Fulham Road in moon boots and jogging pants going "Puss, puss, puss," looking for cats. I hid in a doorway. Please don't tell her where I live.'

Now we were getting close to solving the whole mystery. Candy got hold of a copy of Dolores Cullen's birth certificate and Robin gave me a copy of their wedding certificate. We felt ready for her should she ever re-emerge.

Early one morning Dee phoned Noel when the answering machine was still on and he recorded the conversation by accident.

'I'm sorry to phone so early,' she said, 'but I'm travelling today. Why do you believe all these lies Kathy is spreading about me?' Noel was hardly awake and she kept on berating him so he passed the phone to Candy. 'Hello,' Candy said.

'Who's this?' Dee demanded.

'Candy.'

'It's Dee here.'

Candy was suddenly fully awake. 'Dolores!'

'That's not my name!' Dee snapped.

'Dolores Ann Cullen,' Candy said, 'you used to be married to Robin Clayton.'

'You've got the wrong end of the stick, that's not my name . . .'

'I know what you did to Kathy and Nick.'

'We'll have to do this legally,' she fumed and slammed the phone down. That was the last any of us heard from Diana Bonham-Carter, Dee Clayton, Dee Mitchell, or Dolores Cullen.

One day in 1992 Ronnie Money contacted me out of the blue asking for an address. I was due to go up to London and so I suggested I pop in to visit her in Fulham. She must have mentioned my proposed visit to Chas because he suddenly rang up as well. It was wonderful to hear from him after so long.

We arranged to meet at twelve-thirty and in the end we went on reminiscing and drinking all through the afternoon and well into the evening. We seemed to have so much to talk about. Chas told me he had suffered a burst aorta and nearly died. He was involved in founding the Newcastle Arena, Tyneside's 10,000-seat answer to the Wembley concert venue. But we mostly went over old times. I noticed that he was carrying a lot of weight around the middle – he had always been fond of his beer – but his legs seemed surprisingly thin.

It was still the same old Chas, albeit mellowed with age, still puffing away on cigarettes, his accent as richly Geordie as when he first came down to London. But now, instead of saying he couldn't see how Jimi put up with me, he was saying the opposite. With hindsight he couldn't see how I had been able to put up with Jimi! He remembered our time together very fondly. We parted, promising to keep in touch, and we once dropped in on him in Newcastle on the way up for a visit to Scotland. He was living in a comfortable house in the suburbs near the sea with his wife, Madeleine, a former Miss UK, and his children. He seemed happy and content working on plans to build the arena.

In 1996 I was in London to meet Martin Shankleman, the reporter who was doing a programme for the BBC about Jimi's last days. When his secretary came to get me she told me that Chas had died. 'He was in hospital for tests,' she said. 'They were just about to discharge him but he died in the night.' It seemed unbelievable: Jimi, Angie, Brian, Keith, Mike Jeffery, John Lennon and now Chas. It only seemed the other day that we were all kids together in London and now they had gone.

Noel Redding and I went up to Newcastle for Chas's funeral. When we got there we visited his local pub which was full of familiar faces from his past, mostly from the business side of things. In the church I noticed Jimmy Nail paying his respects and some of the members of Slade, the group he took on after Jimi and turned into a national institution. I sat next to Tony Garland, Jimi's press officer from the sixties, and Madeline Bell's old boyfriend.

'I don't know any of these songs,' Tony was grumbling, 'I'm Jewish.'

'Well, I can't help you,' I muttered back, 'I'm Catholic.'

As we came out of the church I was talking to Hilton Valentine, the lead guitarist from the Animals and John Steel, their drummer, when Noel nudged me in the ribs. 'Al Hendrix is here.'

I looked across and saw a little frail old man. 'What the hell is he doing here?' I wondered aloud. 'He never even knew Chas.'

'Chas had a lot of tapes,' someone said, 'and they want them for their company, Experience Hendrix.'

I remembered back to my meeting with Chas at the Dorchester, when he had kept telling me not to give anything away from my past, to make sure I charged for interviews and that no one else profited from my experiences. I guessed that he had made sure any tapes he had of Jimi at work were well protected.

Al was with his adopted daughter and her husband. One of them recognized me and brought him over and introduced us. He knew who I was as soon as he heard my name.

'We spoke once before,' I said to Al when at last we found ourselves alone together, 'years ago.' He smiled and nodded, not saying anything. 'You told me to tell your son to write because you weren't going to pay for no collect calls!'

'I remember,' he smiled wistfully, 'I remember.'

In 1991 it occurred to me that there should be a 'Jimi Hendrix lived here' Blue Plaque on the house in Brook Street next to Handel's. So that was how, at the opening of this story, I came to be at Brook Street with a crowd big enough to stop the traffic.

I don't consider that the plaque is just for a sixties rock star. It's for all the players in that whirlwind time that destroyed so many and allowed others to survive. Jimi, Brian, Keith and Angie were swept away by it. Many others were badly affected. Poor Monika was a victim of a fan's obsession with rock music and so, in her way, is Dolores Cullen.

My life has become a part of history: a strange feeling, especially when I read about it in other people's words. In these pages, then, I have finally said how I felt about that time. Even with all the weirdness, hilarity, tragedy and mayhem, I wouldn't want to change a line. Whatever else, it *was* fun.